To my friend Lou M.

Gusey O.

2-5-20

Adulting Made Easy(er): Navigating from Campus to Career

Gerry O'Connor, Barbara Schultz, Kimberly White

Adulting Made Easy(er): Navigating from Campus to Career

First published September 2019

Printed in the United States of America.

The Library of Congress has not yet catalogued this book.

Cover Design by Yuke Li

ISBN: 978-0-578-22400-8

Many thanks to our very patient and loving spouses—Ann O'Connor, Marty Schultz, and Benny White—who endured countless hours of alone time as we went about writing this book.

To our children, Niall O'Connor, Andrew Schultz, BJ White, and Logan White, who have proven incredible cheerleaders and sources of younger generation perspectives—thank you for your advice and support throughout the process.

A big shout out to Marti Konstant, Martin McGovern, and Jeff Bruce for your invaluable direction, guidance and overall great insights.

Finally, a very special thank-you to our wonderful editors, D'lynne Plummer and Celia Laskey who helped to get Adulting Made Easy(er) over the finish line.

TABLE OF CONTENTS

INTRODUCTION

Barbara Schultz

This is how our book was born. It all started with Gerry, who sensed a gap in people's financial savvy across all generations and one he could fill with expertise acquired over years as a financial executive. Next, he brought me into the fold to do some brainstorming and see if the idea was big enough or worthy enough to fill the pages of a book. Together we narrowed the scope to a place we believed all financial planning should begin—with smart education and career choices. Enter Kim, who brought better focus by identifying where the greatest need was. After much lively debate, research, and reflection on our collective life/work experiences, Kim served as the tie breaker and helped us understand *who* our readers should be and where we could provide the most value. While it seems obvious now, it wasn't then. We joined hands, turned our attention to the future workforce—Generations Y and Z—and set out to give them all we had to help navigate the course to their first job.

We started by recognizing the forces at play when students are handed a high school diploma, from constantly being asked "So, what are you going to do next?" to managing pressure from parents who feel their alma mater is the *only* choice.

And these same questions will be posed again once kids finish the next level of education and are faced with their first job search. Is Dad expecting them to follow in his footsteps and join the family business? Are parents urging them to just get any job that moves them off their payroll? At these critical moments in life, there's no shortage of people ready to offer advice. It can all be so stressful and confusing!

We considered our next steps and polled friends and colleagues who all gave a collective sigh when considering the resources they wish they had as their kids faced these decisions. We then spoke with a number of kids who confided they felt "lost" and were really enthusiastic about getting advice and maybe even a little surprised at our interest in helping them. As parents and professionals who lived through the same dilemmas and found our way, we knew this was a book we *had* to write.

Our first challenge was bringing clarity to expectations we had of kids and their parents. Our lessons are directed at kids navigating their way from campus to workplace. But we also recognized the journey as a family affair and one that would only succeed with parent's participation and support.

So, we open our book with "the talk" where kids and their parents start a healthy, objective dialogue, discussing the options for educational paths post-high school. Our premise is built on the belief that, in order to enjoy financial success, further education beyond high school will be needed. We promote a number of paths in addition to a four-year degree that include trade schools, certifications, and community college. These choices support the education needed for the diverse careers available in today's dynamic job market.

We identified an often-missed opportunity for kids to take advantage of the wealth of information and guidance available from their support team. That team comprises an entire orbit of people—from parents, teachers, school counselors, network connections, HR professionals, and career coaches. We'll explain how to assemble and when to access your team. We begin with a roadmap, linking self-assessments that lead to smart education and career choices. Every aspect of job seeking is then explored: from the ABC's of résumé writing, personal branding, networking, and interviewing to locating employment opportunities and salary negotiations. Once an offer is accepted, we'll take the mystery out of the work world and explain the importance of demonstrating your potential and value in the first 90 days on the job.

Our combined professional backgrounds make for a powerful database of knowledge, experience and insights. We've all enjoyed success as career coaches, assisting job seekers in developing strategies to land jobs or upgrade roles within organizations. We also share a common bond as parents who helped guide our own kids through the maze of school and career choices.

On an individual basis, Gerry held senior leadership roles in finance, is the savviest of job seekers, and one of the best networkers I know. His strong views of making wise investments in education are carefully detailed with a calculation allowing you to determine the return on investment when choosing a college. He'll take the guesswork out of the decision making with some basic math.

Kim is currently the executive director of a career center whose mission is to empower individuals to seek fulfilling employment. Her daily life is centered on every topic covered in career choice and job search and has earned a great reputation in the community for helping others. She's a big proponent of mentoring and serves as a good model of striking the balance of when to play the role of advisor and parent and when to seek outside help.

And, I have held senior leadership positions in human resources, with an extensive background in talent acquisition and management. I've had the benefit of being on "the other side of the fence" as a hiring manager to lend insight on what happens behind the scenes. With a career spent primarily in entrepreneurial firms, I've developed numerous workforce plans and can now share perspectives related to the knowledge, skills and abilities employers seek.

For students wondering what follows after graduation, here is maybe *the* most important reason to read this book. All three of us understand this critical time in your lives and are committed to making "adulting" easier for you and your parents. We understand the balance needed to help parents "let go" while easing kids down the path of adulting, because we've lived it.

We're excited to share our stories and experiences and are confident these tools and techniques will provide the launch pad for navigating from campus to career. These principles have stood the test of time, so feel free to pick this book up each time you need guidance regarding your education and as you consider a move from one job or career to the next!

CHAPTER 1

"THE TALK"

Gerry O'Connor and Kimberly White

Parents, you want your kids to pursue an education beyond their high school diploma, get on a career track, and leave the nest. But most of all, you want them to be happy and successful. Sounds simple enough, right?

Kids, are you feeling a little stuck and not sure what should happen next? The only thing you figure might be coming is "the talk." That's right, the next conversation you may be facing with your parents is the one about adulting ... and you SO don't want to go there.

In this chapter, we'll bring it all together for both parties so you can agree on an education, training, and career path that works for everyone. We'll explore how to negotiate and reach agreement on the roles everyone plays, so expectations are clear. For kids, we'll help you get unstuck or provide some tried-and-true tips to facilitate the next step forward.

Parents

As parents, you may have already committed to providing financial support either in real dollars, student loan guarantees, or subsidized rent. While you believe in the *concept* of kids exercising independent thinking, you might still view your role as the primary advisor for their future education and career choices. Based on the fact that you've "been there, done that," coupled with your pledge of financial support to the cause (for those in a position to do so), it seems perfectly logical that you would take the lead role in determining their future. After all, who cares more about your kids than you? Consider the dynamics about to unfold as your kids finish high school or prepare to embark on their first job search. The scenario has all the elements of a difficult discussion.[1] Engaging in this dialogue will require preparation and understanding of those dynamics from all parties.

Step one for you is to let go and avoid the temptation to micromanage your student's education and career choices. It might be harder than you thought. On the one hand, you want to encourage independent thinking, but your instincts tell you to be the protector. If you're a financial resource provider (also known as "The Bank of Mom and Dad"), you have the right to expect a return on your investment. The return from your kids may include meeting certain performance standards and conducting diligent education and career research. You, in turn, will give them access to your professional network for advice on future direction and likely will choose to supplement that advice with your personal career experience.

High School Students

For juniors and seniors, your next step may be selecting a college and a major, and the challenge will be to link your education with a career path. Why are you going to college and taking certain courses? Have you researched the types of careers that are supported by your preferred education? Do you know the cost of your proposed education and the likely return on investment (ROI)? Have you had a part-time or summer job to gain work experience and help research career paths? Your parents may be able to help with network sources to research and answer these questions. Chapter 3 addresses how to link education with a future career path.

High School Graduates Considering Alternatives to a Four-Year College

If you know what you want and are taking steps to get there,

---

[1] For guidance on navigating conversations where strong emotions may be involved, I recommend reading *Crucial Conversations: Tools For Talking When Stakes are High* by Kerry Patterson, Joseph Grenny, Ron McMillan, and Al Switzer.

congratulations! You may have decided on a community college, an internship program, an apprenticeship, or you've already landed a job. An associate degree will put you in a better position than a high school diploma for many employment opportunities. Or, once you've had the community college experience, you may decide to transfer to a four-year school rather than starting a career at this time. Whatever academic path you choose, make sure you're always evaluating the investment of time and money alongside the payoff you expect.

If you are feeling a bit lost about your next move after high school and don't want to go to college, your family can help you think through choices concerning your future. Maybe your goal is a job. Maybe you want to be a mechanic. If so, consider an auto-mechanic apprenticeship program. Trial and error will lead you to a place where you enjoy your work and can see a future career. Conduct a Google search for the best jobs available that don't require a college degree.[2]

College Students and Recent Graduates

Maybe you've already decided on a major or have earned a degree and set your sights on an awesome job. Do you know where it leads? If you have a career path in mind, great. Do you know how to navigate your way to that career path? Your parents may be able to help you. If you're not sure what's next after your degree, there are several paths and opportunities to figure it out through family discussions. If your family works in a field related to your desired career, they can introduce you to their network, help with part-time, contract, or intern opportunities, which are all great door openers for the next phase of your career. Before you leave campus, make sure you've explored career fairs and taken advantage of any available career counseling services. If you've already graduated, get involved in your alumni association; there may be some great networking opportunities there.

Coming Together

Remember that "the talk" is a two-way street, so let's look at the roles and responsibilities everyone has in order to make it an effective conver-

---

[2] A list of the 35 best-paying jobs along with the likely vacancies over the next few years can be found here: https://www.thejobnetwork.com/35-high-paying-jobs-with-out-degrees/.

sation. For both parties, an ongoing commitment to regularly and openly communicate about expectations and progress is important.

Parents, I (Kim) highly recommend initiating a career dialogue as soon as your kids start high school. In some cases, your kids might think they know exactly what it is they want to do. In other cases, they might be all over the place, which is okay. The good news is that now is the moment for them to take their time to explore their interests and see which schools might be a match. We took our kids on their respective college tours during the summer between their freshman and sophomore year of high school. They learned a lot about what the schools had to offer relative to their interests. Slowly but surely, education and career paths will emerge. Based on my experience, the earlier you can begin the dialogue, the better. You'll avoid expensive mistakes, wasted time, and possible discouragement.

As most kids do, their initial interests changed. Our son was pursuing political science and ended up with a sociology degree, starting his career as a financial analyst with a firm in New York City. Our daughter was following a path in journalism and ended up with a degree in strategic communications, starting her career with a firm in Washington, D.C. One thing that didn't change was the requirement we put on both of them to continue with their foreign language classes. Our son received a minor in French and our daughter received a minor in Spanish. While they grumbled about taking on the extra course load, we felt learning another language would not only be enriching but would help them be competitive in the job market.

Back in the days before Dot met Com, I (Gerry) chose a college education path linked to a poorly researched career choice. Halfway through my degree, I knew the chosen career path was not for me. The result was a wasted three years getting a degree that I never used. I then had to re-focus my education in a new direction. Luckily, with the support of my family, part-time work, and intensive study, I earned my career-related degree and found a satisfying and rewarding career. Looking back, had I done my career-related research more thoroughly, I could have avoided wasting those three years and the associated added costs.

Focus on the positives as you begin the dialogue. It's about introducing your kids to your professional network, if you have one, that aligns with their career interests and encouraging them to seek advice regarding careers, education tracks, and work opportunities. This stage of networking is addressed in more detail in Chapter 4. Be patient, but persistent. Hold your kids accountable for getting part-time or summer jobs for work experience, while they concurrently conduct career research for the long term.

When having discussions, avoid the use of such timeworn phrases as "when I was your age." Consider an investment in a formal career assessment or encourage utilizing a free career assessment tool such as assessment.com.

Kids, "the talk" can be intimidating unless you know what career path you want and can link it to your education. But it's okay to be a bit lost. Most people have been through this phase of life. Your parents and any older siblings (if any) likely have been there. Ask for their advice on how they researched and selected their career paths. It may have been trial and error, which is a great form of research to identify what you like and dislike about various work environments and experiences. Getting hands-on job experience and learning what motivates you is an invaluable benefit. The earlier you begin a trial and error phase, the better. As you continue a dialogue with your parents, you can also expand your interactions with your developing network of advisors. They can share their experiences, provide objective advice on how they got to where they are, and introduce you to others to continue your research.

My (Gerry's) personal experience as a parent advising kids about their career began when my son was a senior in high school. He didn't know what he was going to do career-wise. While he wanted to go to college, he didn't know what courses he wanted to take. We never had "the talk" about why he wanted to go to college, or what career he might pursue. His first-choice college was expensive. I explained that I'd support him going there if his grades remained above a certain level. He thought about it and decided to consider alternatives. He finally selected a less expensive but reputable college. I told him I expected him to get a part-time job and pay a share of the costs. He did well, graduating in four years with a degree in business and accounting. He also had some useful work experiences.

When I asked what he was going to do with his degree, he told me the only thing he knew for certain is that he wasn't going to pursue a career in either business or accounting! That was when we began "the talk." We worked together to develop a plan for how to research various careers. I introduced him to my network. Our weekly discussions were rigorous. I expected him to make commitments regarding his efforts to network and research. At the end of each week, he reported back on his efforts. We then developed a plan for the next week. After a few months, a member of my network suggested a career path, along with an offer of an entry-level position. My son leaped at the idea and left within days to a 60-hour workweek for no or low pay. He loved it and finally got started on his career path. To this day, he often jokes about our talks but recognizes the career-related benefits of the conversations that got him from where he was to where he wanted to be.

The "Shark Tank" Approach to Career and Education Planning

Kids, if mom and dad are going to invest in your future, let's have a little fun with it by imagining you're an entrepreneur on Shark Tank. You'll have to make a convincing presentation to get their financial support. Consider that you are asking your parents for financial support in the form of money, student loan guarantees, or subsidized rent. Your parents want to know if this is a wise investment.

This popular television show can serve as a great model for how the dynamics between parents and kids could play out. If you're not familiar with the show, here's how it works. An entrepreneur pitches a plan to a group of potential investors, explaining the business model, along with future growth plans. The plan shows the investment needed, along with returns investors can expect. The entrepreneurs share their market research as well as their sales and profit projections. The Q&A happens next, as the investors take a deep dive into the proposed risks and rewards of their potential investments, i.e., what's in it for them? One metric frequently used is the return on investment (ROI). One or more investors may come forward after negotiating acceptable terms with the entrepreneur, or sometimes, the ROI isn't strong enough to interest *any* of the investors. More on that later.

Your Shark Tank story begins with you knowing what you want to achieve, and the investment you want from your parents. Are you ready for your presentation?

To prepare, you'll need to research preferred career paths by meeting with your parents' and your own developing networks, getting part-time work experiences, and, if applicable, using other resources such as career counselors, the campus career office, and job sites. You can then link any required education or training with each potential career path. The combination of research, networking, and work experience can then support your rationale for the school or training you're proposing to acquire for your preferred career path. Your career objective can be interests, compensation, opportunity, inspiration, or other motivators.

The Shark Tank plan outlines what career you want to pursue, how you're going to get there, and the financial investment you are seeking from your parents. From these inputs, you can calculate an ROI. The higher the projected ROI, the more attractive the investment will be.[3]

The inputs necessary to calculate your college ROI are:

A. Expected total cost of college education
B. Expected level of student debt upon graduation
C. Expected earnings in the first year after graduation in your chosen career
D. Expected earnings for the ten years following graduation
E. Expected lifetime earnings in your chosen career

Using the above data, you can calculate the following:

Maximum debt recommended: $B = C$
Ten-Year ROI: D/A (May discount D and A if desired)
Lifetime ROI: E/A (May discount E and A if desired)

What Do These Metrics Tell Us?

If the maximum debt recommended exceeds the expected first-year post-graduation earnings in your preferred career path, examine alternatives to limit your debt level (part-time work, lower-cost colleges, scholarships, etc.) or adjust your preferred career path toward a higher earnings career. If you are comparing various education and career paths, the higher the ten-year ROI, the better the initial education investment. If Plan A has a four-year education costing $120,000, and the expected ten-year earnings is $600,000, the ROI is 5. If Plan B has a similar education cost of $120,000 and generates earnings

---

[3] Robert Farrington of *Forbes* recently wrote a thoughtful article on this topic: https://www.forbes.com/sites/robertfarrington/2019/03/27/how-to-calculate-your-college-education-return-on-investment/#697edf80499c.

of $300,000, the ROI is 2.5. Your "investors" will want to select Plan A unless there are compelling reasons to go with Plan B. Compelling reasons for selecting career paths are more fully discussed in chapter 3.

Get set for the negotiations. You'll be asking investors to commit so you can achieve your career plan. What are you going to give in return? Your first goal is to convince them that the path you've chosen has been well-researched, and you're fully committed. If you are not fully committed, why would anyone want to invest in your plan? You've identified a career path to pursue and the resources needed to get there. These resources can include further education, skills acquisition, mentors, and relevant work experiences. Does your plan outline how you'll acquire these resources? Make sure your plan limits your projected debt load and has a positive ROI.

Your Shark Tank request to your "investors" is for financial assistance and their support of your choices. They will want commitments from you in return. These commitments may include further research to confirm your path, performance levels (grades achieved at a certain threshold) as you pursue your needed education, obtaining summer or part-time work experiences, minimizing student debt, or perhaps getting confirmation of the plan's feasibility from mentors. If they reject your proposal, you need to consider reconfiguring your plan to overcome their objections. The reconfiguration may address a different education or career path, lower investment costs, or require further research.

The Student/Parent Commitment

I (Kim) did have "the talk" with my two kids. I explained that their Dad and I were about to make a significant financial commitment towards their education and wanted to ensure we all had a clear understanding and were on the same page regarding expectations prior to them leaving the nest. As a family, we went through some discussions about education and career planning, and we eventually developed a "Student/Parent Commitment" document. This document is a direct result of conversations I had with other parents whose kids were already in college. Quite frankly, some of what I heard worried me. Our kids are exposed to so much more today than when I was a young person, and I couldn't fathom sending our 18-year-old kids off to school with very little, if any, "rules" to follow. I wanted my kids to have a great college experience, just like other parents, but I wasn't about to let their new-found freedom get in the way of why they were there. The Student/Parent Commitment document put some parameters in place, to ensure my kids would think twice about decisions they made. I thought it important for them to be fully aware of the financial commitment we were making and the expectations we had. I've been asked before if either of my kids broke the commitment contract. Yes, one of them did, and thus incurred additional debt to us because of it.

Below is a modified copy of the document, which should be tailored to fit your family's needs and individual preferences. My kids would be mortified if I listed all of our rules, but let me just say, it helped them to think about choices they were making because of the consequences they would face. My kids agreed to it, lived by it, and graduated with minimal debt. Today, they have awesome jobs in public relations and business, and they're off the family payroll. It worked for me and it might work for you!

The Contract

Providing financial assistance for college is an investment in your future! As long as you agree to the following, and do your part, we will help you achieve your goal of completing college. This is an exciting time for us as a family. This time is an opportunity for you to make new friends, learn from esteemed faculty, and excel in whatever the future has in store for you.

STUDENT'S COMMITMENT

- Call Home
- Work with parents to create a career plan to ensure future success
- Abide by the rules in the University's Code of Conduct
- Attend all classes as scheduled/required
- Ensure parents have access to grades
- Maintain grades at or above agreed grades or those achieved to date
- Manage monthly allowance/finances
- Apply for a credit card or loans only with parent's permission
- Complete an undergraduate degree in four years or less. Any hours above four years will be paid for by student

PARENTS' COMMITMENT/INVESTMENT

We agree to pay for 90% of your tuition/expenses if the above is followed. If we find the student is not following the above, we the parents will decide on the consequence, including but not limited to: immediately stopping all financial support, removing a student from school, and requiring payback from investment previously made.

_____   _____
Student/Date   Parents/Date

The advantage of having a clear contract of commitment is clarity for both parties on their roles and responsibilities. It encourages discussion and regular assessment of performance.

KEY TAKEAWAYS

For Parents

- Start talking about career planning early. It's a long-term process.
- Be supportive and patient to help your student.
- Encourage independent thinking, supported with research.

For the Student

- It's OK to be a bit lost.
- View "the talk" as an opportunity to figure out what you want to do.
- You have lots of supporters willing to advise.
- Don't be reluctant to ask for help as you research education and career choices.

For All

- You'll be more effective as a team working towards a common goal.
- Keep talking about this subject. It's the best way to learn.

CHAPTER 2

THE EVOLVING CAREER PLAN

Kimberly White

We're living in a different and challenging time, unlike anything the previous generations encountered. Our kids can explore the internet and question their parents on absolutely everything we tell them. They can Google and fact-check us in the blink of an eye, so we'd better have our answers ready.

We all want the same things for our kids: for them to grow up happy, healthy, and successful, but we often assume we know exactly what that means for them. In fact, we may figure they'll aspire to the same things our parents had in mind for us: to grow up to be productive citizens in their communities, help those who are in need and, one day, give us grandchildren.

As parents, we need to reset our notion of the perfect life we want for our kids. Even with the best intentions, we might be setting unrealistic expectations that will only lead to disappointment for both them and us. Now is the time to acknowledge that our perceptions of the perfect marriage, the perfect lawn, and perfect children who make the perfect grades may hold a totally different value for our kids.

Our aspirations might be unattainable or undesirable in their eyes and may ultimately only serve to alienate them from us. So, let's all take a deep breath and accept that every path we've chosen may not be the right ones for our kids. Our kids are blessings to us and have distinct personalities, interests, talents, and dreams. The best gift we can give them is sharing our wisdom. We can then help guide them on their journey to happiness and success, even if it's not exactly what we had in mind. Here are five things needed to establish the evolving career plan, including the roles played by parents, kids, mentors, counselors, and connections in their networks.

Encourage Individual Paths to Success

One size does not fit all. Kids are influenced by opinions on so many fronts—parents, teachers, friends, counselors—and may not have formed their own view of the future. Our responsibility as parents is to help guide them toward smart decisions, rather than simply impose on them what worked for us. We may also be tempted to steer them away from choices we made in the past, which while not fatal were also less than optimal. In both cases, our responsibility now is to pass on our knowledge, be open and available to listen to their ideas, and respect their decisions. They won't always succeed the first time (just as we didn't), but with our guidance, they'll learn and develop their own sensibility along the way.

Following High School, Is College the Only Choice?

Unfortunately, most high school systems promote a single solution for graduating seniors: college is the next and only destination! Not every kid is meant to go to college, just like not all kids have the right DNA for professional sports. Some kids have amazing mechanical skills and understand how things work. Who remembers Mike? Mike, who sat next to you in fourth-period math class. Mike, who wanted nothing more than the bell to ring so he could head to auto-shop class. Auto shop was where Mike thrived. It was a place he could get his hands dirty, play under the hood, and tinker with wires until he finally heard the slow start of the car. Yes, this was Mike's happy place!

Parents, your most important job is to steer your kids in the direction that is meant for them. By now, we have some insights into their strengths and weaknesses, know their interests and dislikes, and know (or have an inkling) if they want to be a doctor or tinker with cars.

Choosing whether to go to a two-year college, four-year college, or trade school should be viewed as equally viable options for students. Pursuing a trade (welding, electrical, plumbing, auto mechanic, etc.) is an excellent way for some students to make a great living, and parents need to encourage this choice. Once the path forward becomes more apparent, parents and their kids should work together to create an action plan, set goals, and identify a mentor.

Create an Action Plan

An action plan is an individualized plan to help kids identify career goals and start with steps needed to achieve those goals. By creating a plan, your kids will learn more about their interests and passions, which can then align with career choices. The next step is to gauge skill sets and education requirements needed for specific jobs. The action plan will help guide your kids to:

- Find their passion
- Have effective and productive conversations with teachers and guidance counselors
- Identify education and skill gaps between what they have today and what they'll need to get for the job they want
- Differentiate themselves from others

You may also want to consider a more formal inventory of their talents by purchasing assessment instruments, which could prove a worthwhile investment.

So, time to get your kids working on "writing their own ticket" to the future. You can start with a simple plan at no cost but the investment of time. The more detail they can provide, the better the plan. The initial plan doesn't need to include all the components listed below, but to get started, encourage them to complete the first four items on the list.

As their education and career research progresses, they can access their network to research and complete the remaining topics. Get them involved in answering these questions and gathering the following information:

Step 1: Write the initial plan

1. What is my ideal role and how do I get there?
2. Do I have a résumé that clearly identifies my current skills?
3. What are my current skills and experience, and what's needed to address any gaps?
4. What are the opportunities in my chosen career path?

5. How do I differentiate myself with education, work experiences, and job skills?
6. Do I have a network of advisors to provide counsel on the plan and progress made?
7. What value can I provide to prospective employers?
8. Can I adapt to market changes? Are my skills current?
9. How do I build a brand to showcase my capabilities to prospective employers?
10. How do I get the job I want and how will I be ready for the opportunity?
11. Am I meeting my career goals?

Step 2: Monitor the plan and update it as needed, but at least annually

1. Am I on track to meet my one-year and five-year career goals? If not, what corrective action is required?
2. Have my life goals changed since the last career plan?
3. Have I added skills or accomplishments to my résumé this past year?
4. Have I identified gaps in my education, skills, and experiences that need to be addressed?
5. Have I recently surveyed the latest opportunities in my chosen career field?
6. Is the macro marketplace for my skills and experiences changing? Am I keeping current?
7. Have I found the best environment for my career in terms of culture, mission, industry, and role?
8. What unique career attributes have I gained to make me stand out in my chosen career path?
9. Have I consulted my "inner circle" network for input on my career plan?
10. Is my network effective and have I refreshed it recently? Do I need to add more members?
11. Am I adding value in my current position? Can I quantify the value added?
12. Am I communicating my skills and value to my network and the general marketplace?
13. Are my job-search skills current and effective?
14. Have I updated my plan using a SWOT analysis—reviewing my strengths, weaknesses, opportunities, and threats?

S.M.A.R.T. GOALS

When your kids can identify life goals and integrate them into a plan, they'll have a greater chance at enjoying a successful career. Their career goals should be modeled after S.M.A.R.T goals:

- Specific: covers the who, what, when, where, and why of the plan
- Measurable: makes the goal tangible by listing milestones of progress
- Attainable: focuses on the achievable to encourage inspiration and motivation
- Relevant: keeps you on track with what makes sense and is realistic
- Time-based: includes target dates for deliverables

Help guide your kids to set these goals—mentors, counselors, and teachers can also be involved. Career goal setting is imperative as they visualize the future. The first step is to help them establish long-term goals. Once those are established, then set short-term goals in one, three, and five-year increments to reach the ultimate goals. Don't overlook the need to also identify and address barriers to accomplishing their goals.

Identify a Mentor

This is a job for your kids to take on. A mentor is someone they look up to, maybe aspire to be, and absolutely have a great chemistry with—that's the most important component.

Mentors can come from all areas of your life and they play a vital role in shaping career paths. A mentor is a confidant and supporter who helps navigate a career journey with problem-solving techniques and professional development tips. A trusted individual who's not a parent can provide objective direction and advice and can be especially helpful with personal and professional highs and lows. The advice mentors pull from their breadth of experience offers something more than a Google search. Of course, parents will always be trusted advisors, as you want nothing but the best for your kids. However, having an industry-specific mentor as part of a "dream team" is key to their future success.

Understanding the available tools as well as who should play what role are equally important elements of launching your kids into adulting. Make sure your kids take advantage of the combined knowledge and experience of all the people in their world of connections. And, be sure to share in the collective wisdom.

KEY TAKEAWAYS

- Work with your kids to create a plan that will lead to future success.
- Know your kids—don't force them into the career YOU want for them. Instead, help to guide them as they find a career that works for them!
- A good mentor knows what success looks like and will help to empower their mentees to make informed and impactful choices. Encourage your kids to find one!

CHAPTER 3

THE ROADMAP: GETTING ON THE RIGHT PATH

Gerry O'Connor

"Tell me what it is you plan to do
With your one wild and precious life?"
—Mary Oliver, poet

You may be a high school senior, a college student, a recent college graduate, or engaged in work-related training. You may have some ideas about the direction you want to take to get educated and start your career. You may be a bit lost. It's okay. This chapter can be your guide as you research where you want to go in life.

Your mom wants you to be a brain surgeon while your dad thinks you'd make a perfect accountant. Now throw in the fact that you've got plans that are different from them about what's next in your life. Maybe they don't understand you're looking to join Google as a web engineer and launch the next app that changes the world?

Members of your family can play a role as your first post-high-school career advisors. They know you and care about you, making for a great combination to help launch you to the next stage of your life. But the only way it will successfully play out is if you're all on the same page about education and career choices.

To land your dream job, you'll first need to identify an educational path that's going to get you there. We'll help kick off the process by providing a template for you and your family to work together toward that goal.

Life after high school can feel like you're heading for the great unknown, so where do you start? Does it make sense to figure out what kind of education or training you'll need? Have you already mapped out your next career move and know what additional training you'll need to get the job? Maybe you've discovered an entry-level job where the employer will offer in-house training once you start.

These are a few of the preliminary decisions to make, so why not have a roadmap to help get you there?

Start at the Beginning

Start with a simple assessment of who you are today, what you might aspire to in the future, and how you might get there. Here may be some questions you're contemplating for the first time. This template is intended to get you thinking, help shape your identity, and lead you to better decisions.

The first thing is to perform a self-assessment of who you are today in terms of education level, work skills and experiences, and personal skills and adaptability. The key questions are:

- What education do I have today, e.g., high school, some college, preferred subjects?
- What are my work experiences, including everything from lifeguard to landscaper?
- What are my work skills, e.g., punctuality, accepting responsibility, collaboration?
- What are my personality traits, e.g., empathy, patience, collegiality?

The best way to do this is to ask your family and others who know you well for their perspectives. As you progress in building out a professional network, you will get a broader level of input, and your assessment will improve.

The second step is to outline what you might want from your work life in the future. Getting to this point is a process, rather than a one-off exercise. The step begins with family discussions and expands as you network with others to get their advice (see chapter 4). Key questions to research include:

- What work-life balance do I want, e.g., do I work to live, or live to work?
- What general career paths are appealing, e.g., IT, coding, engineering, medicine?
- Is financial security important to me, e.g., do I focus only on high paying careers?
- Is job security important to me, e.g., do I focus only on more stable careers?

As you begin to formulate a preferred working environment and some general career preferences, the final step is to consider these questions:

- What are job opportunities within my general career preferences?
- What skills are needed, and how will I acquire them?
- Who has specific knowledge regarding my career preferences with whom I can network?
- Do my career preferences meet my compensation or job security needs?

The above assessments are helpful for you to identify what you have today, what you will need to get to your destination, and the gaps you need to address. The most important step is to identify your objectives, whether they're acquiring money, prestige, power, respect, social justice, or having it all. Figure out what motivates you, and the rest will follow. Invest the time upfront to do your research and answer these questions as you plan for the next phase of your life. Each question is discussed in more detail later in the chapter.

1. Who or what inspires me to emulate their achievements?
2. What changes do I anticipate in the workplace and education over the next five years?
3. What work experiences will help me land my first real job? What kind of summer, part-time, or internship positions are available?
4. How can I start building a network of people to advise me on education and career choices? Is there anyone in that network willing to act as a mentor?
5. Can I link my career choice to an education plan, or link an education plan to my career choice?

6. Have I considered education and training alternatives?

Inspirations

Inspiration can come from anywhere or anyone. First, look inside your inner circle of family and friends and consider anyone you've admired; explore their work/life experience. You don't have to limit yourself to close connections; your role model for success could be a celebrity or media personality.

Your inspiration may not even come from a person. It may start with interests in a social movement, artistic endeavor, political cause, etc. In all cases, do your homework and take a deeper dive into the stories behind how people in those fields achieved their goals. Research those causes to which you feel drawn and understand the job opportunities in those fields. It's okay to dream big if the path to the goal has some likelihood of success. It's not enough to "imagine it, and they will come." You'll have to work hard to turn goals into reality.

It's equally important to identify the careers that have zero appeal to you. People can sometimes make choices based solely on the compensation package and ignore their inner voice telling them a particular path is wrong.

Are your parents pressuring you to pursue a career path without really hearing your concerns? Or, maybe you feel pushback from your friends who want you to follow them to the college they chose.

Just as there are people who help move you forward, there may also be people and circumstances that put you at a standstill, or, even worse, set your plans on a backward slide. These barriers can take on many forms, from parental and peer pressure to your fear of the unknown or maybe even financial barriers—for example, if a career path cannot pay enough to live *and* repay a student debt. With all these forces potentially impacting your future, the best way to determine your fate is to get ahead of it all and put a plan in place.

Start by making a list of your top five areas of interest. The list will serve as a baseline; you'll then do additional research before coming to any conclusion about the next steps. Use the list to initiate a conversation with your family, teachers, career counselors, and anyone else you can find as you seek career advice. Creating relationships with these people is the beginning of networking.

Hobbies and extracurricular activities can serve as a good starting point to identify areas that might be of interest for a future career. For example, if you love to watch basketball and think about relaying the play-by-play, a career as a sportscaster may be worth considering. Or, if you love the analytics behind the game, the field of data analytics could be your happy place. You might even research a career in sports retailing, perhaps as a buyer for a big-box retailer.

The point is, there are endless choices, and you'll need to narrow them down with the help of some good research, assistance from family and friends, and by talking with people in your network who have "been there, done that."

Workforce Trends

Technology is in perpetual motion, and you'll need to keep pace with it. The workplace changes almost daily, so understanding the impacts of these changes is important to your research. Being aware of the likely impacts of artificial intelligence, 5G, social media, machine robotics, etc., is critical to selecting a career path. Actively managing your career enables you to keep a watchful eye on both the opportunities and the risks.

What *are* the jobs of the future? You can Google "jobs of the future" and find a wealth of information. A favorite site of mine is JFF (jff. org), which has several thoughtful articles on young people entering the workforce and identifying alternative career paths. Another is the Bureau of Labor Statistics Occupational Outlook Handbook (bls.gov/ooh/) that reflects projected job growth by category from 2014-2024. The updated Handbook is essential reading for anyone wanting to make sure that jobs are waiting for them.

What about utilizing the expertise of a professional career coach or counselor? One group I came across, earlystagecareers.com, has expanded the traditional career counseling role to include coaching, mentoring, and placement services. While career counseling may be expensive, career assessment tests are a less costly way to identify areas of aptitude and interests (more on this in chapter 5).

Work Experiences

Summer jobs, part-time jobs, and internships provide a chance to identify the jobs and work environments that might match your goals (in addition to giving you the first taste of financial freedom). You'll gain an understanding of the dynamics involved working with and for others while solving problems—great skills to take with you to any future employer. Take advantage of learning all you can about the business and the industry sector. You can begin building relationships with co-workers who may form the start of your first professional network.

To find these opportunities, use your family, your network, and search online at job sites geared to your job search criteria. Internships often provide the best chance to "test the waters" and learn if the organization or career path is suitable. Unlike summer or part-time jobs, employers often view internships as a pipeline for future, permanent employees. If you perform well during the internship process, an employer may even make an offer in advance of your graduation, securing a spot for you in their organization. While many internships pay little or nothing, the value to you is in the work experience and contacts.

While a first job is important, initial job exploration is a trial-and-error process as you search for your sweet spot. Ask baby boomers or Gen X'ers how they started on a career path and they'll likely recount it as a long and winding road of experimentation and varied jobs. Now is the time to research alternatives with summer and part-time jobs and internship before you make a longer-term commitment.

Networking

Networking is where you gather career knowledge and identify opportunities.

If you are a high school senior, your network is likely limited to family, friends, teachers, and neighbors. This group represents the starting block for any network. In chapter 4, you will learn how to build out your network with people who have the expertise and background to help you research and select your career path.

If you are already in college and unsure of what you want to do next, you can get excellent advice from your network. By now, your network will have expanded to include fellow students, faculty, the college career office, and maybe your college alumni.

If you are a recent college graduate but still unsure of how to get started on a career path, your network can introduce you to alternative careers and opportunities. Be sure to stay in touch with your alumni association. They will be an excellent source of advice and help you identify opportunities.

If you are already working or engaged in work-related training and are seeking greater opportunity, your network is the best path to finding more desirable work.

Networking is out of the comfort zone for even the most seasoned workers who anticipate the awkwardness of "asking a favor" from someone they may or may not know very well. Although it can feel uncomfortable at first, the only way to build a network is to get out there and meet people. Nine out of ten times you'll be pleasantly surprised at the welcome reception you receive. Almost everyone in the workplace has benefitted from networking and is very happy to be able to "return the favor."

Networks can also be a source of potential mentors who can help secure suitable seasonal or part-time exploratory jobs and later may provide more specific guidance about various industries, career choices, and educational paths.

Educational Choices

Linking education and career is a common concern. Should you select an educational path to fit a desired career, or pursue an educational path with the hope, it will lead to a career? If you know you want to be a web designer, then you can choose the appropriate college courses. If earning potential is your end game and the specific academic course is less important, you can identify the degrees expected to provide the highest compensation. The World Economic Forum prepared an analysis linking various degrees to future compensation.[4]

If you have a career path in mind, it is relatively straightforward to identify and pursue the required educational needs to get on the chosen career path. You can confirm your educational needs by networking with people who have been successful in your chosen career. If you have selected an educational path, greater research is needed to find a selection of possible career paths. Here is where you need to examine what you are passionate about and what inspires you. You can research jobs of the future and get summer and part-time work experience. Seek out possible intern opportunities in various organizations. Access your network for advice on career paths associated with your educational path.

[4] https://www.weforum.org/agenda/2018/07/which-college-degrees-get-the-highest-salaries

Is a Four-Year College Degree for You?

A college degree can provide a pathway to higher lifetime earnings. A recent book by Richard Vedder, *Restoring the Promise*, notes that 30% of Americans hold college degrees, but the modern economy doesn't possess the number of jobs commensurate with the expectations of all the degree-holders.

What are the monetary benefits of obtaining a college degree? The best way to assess these is to compute a Return on Investment (ROI), as discussed in chapter 1. A useful website for further ROI analysis is Bankrate (bankrate.com).

While a degree may provide higher compensation, the absolute benefit as compared to other educational paths is declining for several reasons. All careers require that workers are agile. Many modern careers in tech and manufacturing require ongoing skill updates rather than one four-year term. Employers are not only seeking skills that can be learned but are also looking for abilities such as problem-solving, critical reasoning, collaboration, creativity, and empathy, rather than a specific degree. These skills can come from work experiences.

The high cost of a four-year degree can outweigh the benefits unless the degree opens a path to a high-paying career. Finally, the data ignores the fact that 40% of people who pursue a four-year degree course fail to graduate within six years and are likely to experience disappointment and the burden of student debt.

According to the National Center for Education Statistics:

- 36% of four-year college students graduate in four years
- 60% of four-year college students graduate in six years or less

What happens to the 40% who don't graduate in six years? They lose a significant amount of self-confidence and gain a hefty student debt load. Choose carefully.

Research has shown that it's not what college you attend, but what you do at college that is the best predictor of career success. Use the internet to research various colleges that teach you how to acquire and build skills in problem-solving, critical reasoning, collaboration, creativity, and empathy. Be sure to check out the level of career guidance and support provided by the college career counseling services. Also look at the non-academic opportunities provided by each college that encourage relationship building, trying new things, risk-taking, and other forms of creative development.

Is a Two-Year Community College an Option?

An associate degree provides a lower-cost alternative to a four-year degree and can be completed in two years. If you decide to continue your academic studies, you can then use the credits earned and apply them toward a four-year degree. Amazon, Google, IBM, and other companies are using community colleges as a significant pipeline to attract and develop talent pools, according to the *Wall Street Journal*.[5]

Are Vocational Training and Apprenticeship Programs an Alternative?

Vocational training focuses on specific knowledge and skills needed for trades, crafts, and an ever-growing list of other careers. This form of training includes operational training in retail, hospitality, tourism, property management, computer services, healthcare coding, and many other categories.

Online trade programs offer high school graduates an excellent opportunity to earn a trade accreditation while maintaining flexibility and completing certification in a shorter time than with on-campus attendance. There are numerous programs available in which you can receive training for your trade of choice. These include animal care, carpentry, electrical, forestry and wildlife, home inspection and plumbing.

Consider searching available apprenticeships in your areas of interest, such as mechanic, carpenter, electrician, and court reporter. An apprenticeship provides an immediate paying job, coupled with job-related education and skills training. The final credential provides a pathway to career advancement and job security.[6]

Many of these opportunities are not well-publicized and may only be accessible through your network.

---

[5] https://www.wsj.com/articles/big-techs-hot-new-talent-incubator-community-college-1530277200

[6] https://www.apprenticeship.gov/become-apprentice

What about a Gap Year?

If you're not feeling ready to pack your bags and head off to college, consider a gap year. A gap year can take you away from the pressures of having to make college and career decisions before you are ready, and it can help avoid costly mistakes. It enables you to travel and get jobs that pay the bills and give you valuable work experience. You can use part-time and other short-term work experiences to help narrow your career choices.

Work experience is perhaps the best source of career path guidance. All jobs provide some learning regarding what you like and dislike. The values learned include discipline, personal responsibility, and hard work. The skills acquired include taking direction, conflict resolution, teamwork, and efficiency. You will learn what you don't like, such as being micro-managed, boredom and repetition, lack of or too much customer interaction, or limited skill-learning opportunities. Get a job in your preferred area, such as office work, auto mechanics, or hospitality, and use the experiences gained to guide your career direction going forward. When you augment work experience with periodic training and further education, your skills remain up-to-date, and your career opportunities broaden. But be careful. The downside of a gap year is that you might not return to an educational path and end up in a dead-end job. Make sure you develop a plan to get your career on track.

My early work experiences taught me some valuable skills. I learned what work environments I liked, and those I wanted to avoid. I worked in the hospitality industry as a waiter, front office supervisor, and bookkeeper. I liked the collaborative process of working in a team. I liked being rewarded for work well-done. I learned that I was motivated by earning the esteem of my co-workers and customers. I sought autonomy, where I controlled my work environment. Finally, I wanted mobility to take my new skills into other roles. These experiences have always guided my career direction.

KEY TAKEAWAYS

- The earlier you begin the process of researching careers, the better. Your research begins with discussing choices and scoping out research with your family and teachers.
- Understanding who or what inspires you will guide your

research. Network with people who can advise on career and educational direction and identify opportunities in areas where you have an interest.

- Get work experiences in areas that will contribute to your research. These experiences will teach you a lot about yourself, especially your preferred work environments.
- Networking is the number one source of information in career research. Meeting people who are in careers provides you valuable information regarding their experiences and the opportunities that are there for you.
- When selecting a post-high school education path, understand what your objectives are. If you don't know what you want to do, consider lower-cost alternatives to a four-year college track.

CHAPTER 4

NETWORKING: CREATING YOUR TEAM

Gerry O'Connor

Do you think of networking like a visit to the dentist's office? Asking the advice of total strangers may not top your list of things you can't wait to do. But unfortunately, you can't wait—especially if you're going to get your career off to a great start. I'll show you how to approach networking opportunities with confidence by supplying tools to develop and maintain connections. Maintaining those connections and building new ones throughout your career are among the most valuable investments you can make for continued professional success Let's start with the kind of communication needed when it comes to building those networking relationships. People from your generation have grown up, relying heavily on mobile devices. After all, cell phones are super-efficient when it comes to getting in touch quickly. However, when it comes to building a network, the value of looking someone in the eye and establishing a personal bond cannot be overstated.

The first step in networking is to identify and cultivate a group of business and professional associates for mutual benefit. Once mastered, the art of networking provides connections who can offer career guidance, market intelligence, and job search support to achieve your career goals.

Here's a real-life scenario of my son's first experiences with networking. As a college senior, he began talking with several of my friends and business associates; looking for general direction feedback, rather than focusing on information related to their specific positions or industries. During the research, he met several people in different professional fields. These discussions were invaluable, as they led to his first milestone decision to pursue a job in public service, rather than in corporate America. Once he figured out his general direction, he took more time with his ever-expanding network to figure out how to get to where he wanted to be. Slowly and surely, those conversations showed him a path that he was able to follow. His network helped him learn the specific education and training required to get a foothold in public service. They helped him select a master's degree course and college. They guided him regarding the most appropriate entry-level positions to pursue. Today he is an expert networker, regularly seeking advice and returning the favor, assisting others in their career or job search.

Developing Your First Network

Why network? Because that's where you get access to career advice, market intelligence, and job opportunities. Upwards of 80% of positions are identified and secured through effective networking.

As you work on identifying what or who inspires you, and what your passions and interests are, the next step is to begin talking with people who can expand your knowledge. Building your network starts with identifying people who are engaged in careers or industries that interest you, or people whom you consider both knowledgeable and approachable about careers in general. Your family, co-workers, high school teachers, college professors, college alumni, and friends are all likely early-stage sources to introduce you to prospective network members.

As you identify a person of interest, add them to your network list. Contact each person on the list by phone or e-mail, introducing yourself and referencing whoever provided you with their name. Begin by explaining that you are in the process of reviewing careers and would welcome their advice. Indicate your flexibility to meet at a place and date suitable to your contact. Once you have arranged a meeting, try to learn about your connection. LinkedIn is an excellent resource to provide career details of the person, including job title, industry, employer name, and other information. Look out for items in their backgrounds that are of interest to you.

Be curious. Before the meeting, draw up a series of questions you wish to ask the contact during the session. The items can address their professional backgrounds, their process of selecting a career or education path, any mistakes learned in their career selection processes, along with opportunities in their industries for people like you. Ask open-ended questions about what advice they can provide as you set out on your career research. Finally, and most importantly, ask if they are willing to introduce you to others to continue your research. For each networking meeting, dress professionally, and be respectful of their time. When in doubt, dress up, not down, introduce yourself, and explain where you are in the process of researching career paths. Ideally, have your introduction (your elevator speech – see chapter 7) written out and rehearsed before the meeting. Do not hesitate to indicate you are unsure of a path and in need of lots of advice. During the meeting, ask your prepared questions and listen carefully to the answers. Ask if you may take notes during the discussion but do so sparingly. A key question is who they can introduce you to for additional research. Discuss how you should contact each person recommended. If the meeting has been successful in terms of good advice or further contacts, ask if you may follow up in a few weeks to review progress and ask more questions. Finally, ask if you may connect through LinkedIn going forward. Assembling a collection of LinkedIn contacts provides a useful set of people for further research and communication.

Be grateful. After each meeting, make notes of information learned. Send a thank-you e-mail to each person you meet, indicating you will provide them with information regarding your progress. Make sure you retain the notes for future follow-up.

Engaging in this type of networking helps build an ecosystem of career advisors who you can access with more specific questions as your career research progresses. People enjoy helping others, especially those who are beginning their careers and seeking educational advice. So, do not hesitate to ask for help. Everyone with a career has experienced the concerns of getting started, and in almost all cases, wish to share their experiences and knowledge to help others.

Keep in mind that the essence of successful networking is not, "What can I get?" but rather "how may I help." As you accumulate knowledge and experience, you can then give back to others who are starting on the same road. Do not be afraid of introducing yourself and seeking advice. Nine times out of ten, you'll be pleasantly surprised at the welcome reception you receive.

Guidelines

Effective networking is preferably a face-to-face exercise. Every meeting is an opportunity to network. Every business and social event or gathering is an opportunity to network. These initial introductory meetings may be supplemented with individual follow-up sessions that can focus on identifying mutual career experiences and research needs. Once a connection is made, you have successfully added a person to your network.

As you meet people in a work environment, either co-workers or business acquaintances, consider if they have the experience and background that can assist you in your career research or job search. Ask yourself if these people may be able to provide advice and contacts. If the answer is yes, ask for a meeting to introduce yourself, explaining your career-related needs. In other words, present your elevator speech.

Business gatherings offer excellent venues to identify connections. These gatherings span a wide variety of meeting types, including subject-matter conferences, professional groups, job fairs, college alumni meetings, and conventions. While there is an opportunity to meet several people within a short period, you may also have limited one-on-one access to have in-depth conversations. The real value in this type of venue is the face-to-face time that can translate into a follow-up meeting.

The way to keep the door open with people you've met is to exchange business cards and commit to following up. If you're a student, the card should have contact information, including mobile number, e-mail, LinkedIn address, and may include a headshot. Business cards are a low-cost investment, available online through companies like Vistaprint, or purchased at office supply retail stores for a nominal price. Keep the connection active with a timely follow-up by e-mail to arrange a face-to-face or phone meeting.

Networking events offer an efficient way to meet several people over a short period. Topics covered in those meetings are usually either specific to job functions (accounting, engineering, human resources) or may address workforce trends (pluses and minuses of open office concepts, employee benefits). How do you approach a group of people engaged in a conversation at such an event? My method has been to join the group and listen to the conversation until I see an opening for me to contribute. Within five or ten minutes, I've become part of the conversation. As time permits, I can then introduce myself and ask others in the group to do the same.

Picture the "speed dating" model, and you'll understand how to have a one-on-one meet and greet in a relatively short space of time. Attendees can provide a one or two-minute elevator speech and solicit feedback from others. I usually set a goal to meet and connect with at least ten people at these types of events. Other attendees may have decided to reach out to me. Overall, I may have accumulated at least fifteen connections for future communications and possibly one-on-one meetings. Pretty good results for spending just a few hours of my time to expand my network!

Social gatherings can also serve as networking events. Weddings, family gatherings, faculty-student gatherings, and alumni meetings all fall within this category. Usually, there is more time to get to know each other and talk about careers and backgrounds. Meeting possible network members at such events is more relaxed as there are two common ties: the links to the event organizer and shared experiences. Again, make a timely follow-up to arrange a face-to-face meeting. Have a disciplined approach, and you've got a much better chance of reaching your goals. Be realistic about the time it takes to make the initial contact, meet, do follow-up calls, and connect with new introductions. I usually try to target an actual number of connections and sessions per month. If you're a recent college grad, you'll want to establish career research meetings and job-search goals to ensure a higher volume of activity. Spend your time calling on your existing network and adding new contacts. If you're exclusively using the internet for research and responding to job postings by applying online, then you're bypassing the most significant sources of career advice and jobs.

If you're still enrolled in school or college and conducting informational meetings or seeking general career advice, a less aggressive schedule of contacting people will probably make sense. You've got the benefit of time and don't share the same sense of urgency as someone in active job search mode.

The Meeting

Call or e-mail your prospective network member asking to meet over coffee or lunch close to their place of work. If they live in another geographic location, ask for a telephone or video conference meeting. Explain the purpose of the meeting. It's okay to say the objective is to help you research your career choices, goals, and opportunities. Prepare a list of customized questions touching on the expertise of the other person. Be prepared to discuss your background, your aspirations, and how the other person can assist you.

At the meeting, introduce yourself using your elevator speech. Ask your prospective network member for their career status and experiences. For each question you ask, consider providing the same information about yourself in return. You may bring your résumé to the meeting or offer to send it later. A key takeaway from these meetings is obtaining introductions to other people to continue to grow your network.

After the meeting, it is useful to make notes of your discussion, and any action items agreed. Often a follow-up meeting is arranged. If you are offered introductions to others, send another e-mail to arrange details about how to make contact.

Here's a checklist of useful takeaways when attending a networking meeting:

- Research the background of people you'll be meeting. LinkedIn is an excellent resource for this.
- Establish and research your goal(s) for each session: Advice? Introductions? Planting a seed?
- Prepare questions related to what you are seeking.
- Practice your presentation, especially your elevator speech and your Q&A.
- Be on time for your meeting.
- Be professional, which includes dressing appropriately.
- Be clear about your goals at the onset of the meeting.
- Offer to "pay it back." For example, if your contact supports a not-for-profit, volunteering is a way to reciprocate.
- Be calm and confident. Good preparation helps.
- Share your business card.
- Offer to provide your résumé.
- Ask for introductions to others who may be able to help.
- Do more listening than talking and engage in "active" listening— say things like, "That makes sense," or "That's great advice."
- Follow up with a thank-you e-mail.

Have a Specific Plan Tailored to Every Type of Networking Event

Here are some networking tips and techniques used by a colleague seasoned in the art of networking. His experience reflects an advanced skill set in the art of networking and is included to demonstrate how his methods are useful as you advance in your career. His goal is to introduce his consulting business capabilities and recent successes, seeking out market intelligence to identify opportunities for his services. He has successfully grown his business primarily through effective networking and spends minimal time or money on any other form of marketing. Follow in his footsteps as he "works the crowd" at a networking event and consider using these tips:

- He wants to know who will be attending the event and their business backgrounds. A method he uses is to call the event organizer to say he is considering attending but would like to know who else will be there. Usually, the organizer will be helpful, providing at least the names of participating organizations and often the names of several individuals. Noting the names and backgrounds of event speakers also indicates the types of attendees.

- He looks for attendees he might know and who can assist in introducing him to others.
- He wears appropriate business attire for the event.
- He ensures he has business cards and a small notebook to jot down vital information immediately after the event or useful individual discussions.
- He arrives early to familiarize himself with the meeting format. He also hopes to get further information on attendees. Usually, names of attendees are available at the entrance to the meeting.
- He may ask the event organizer to make introductions to participants he wants to meet.
- He introduces himself to other attendees before the event gets busy.

His approach is to introduce himself by name, job title, and what he does. He asks the same of the other person. All the time, he's seeking shared interests and backgrounds. If a follow-up get-together is agreed, he'll exchange business cards and arrange for further communication. For specific people he wishes to meet, he'll have someone point them out and make a beeline to them. Throughout the event, he may introduce himself to twenty or more people, and arrange follow-up communications with ten.

Your "Inner Circle"

A significant purpose of your network as you begin your career is to seek out initial advisors who can provide constructive career guidance and help to secure seasonal or part-time exploratory work. These advisors can guide you regarding industries, careers, skill gaps, and educational paths. This group, your "inner circle," begins to grow once you have entered the workforce. Ideal members are fellow employees and professional friends who are experiencing similar career patterns, and with whom you can both give and take constructive career advice regarding opportunities, challenges, and career development needs. This tight circle of four or five members can frequently meet as a single group or as sub-groups. Over time, membership of your "advisory board of directors" may change as individual needs and contributions begin to move in different directions.

My inner circle has five members. The first three have worked with me in the past, and we have stayed in touch. The final two members are recent additions who have senior management backgrounds and who are at the midpoint of their careers. They bring more recent millennial and Gen X perspectives. All of them know me very well and can act as sounding boards for my career ideas. They provide constructive suggestions and criticisms, each of which is invaluable. In building my inner circle, I often seek complementary skills and experiences to my own, so I get fresh perspectives and new ideas on how to address challenges.

Finding A Mentor

A mentor is a person who provides a younger or less experienced person help and advice over time regarding education and career guidance. A mentor should be someone you can look up to, who inspires you and responds to your questions. How do you find an effective mentor? Networking is an activity that helps you identify possible mentors. As you conduct networking meetings, you'll notice some people are more knowledgeable, more helpful, or more in tune with your research. Following up on your initial networking meeting, send a thank you note and request a follow-up meeting to expand your career and education research. If the second meeting is going well, consider asking them to become your mentor. Your expectations of a mentor are that they will be available regularly, perhaps every two or three months, to discuss and critique your career and education direction. Bear in mind that an effective mentor will challenge you. They will provide honest feedback. Some of this interaction may be uncomfortable. Accept it as part of having a constructive dialogue. Mentoring is a long-term process that depends on your mentor learning about you and giving you honest feedback. The process also depends on your consideration of your mentor's advice. Think of your mentor to be your "go-to" person whom you can rely on to give you their full attention and unvarnished opinions.

Your "Outer Circle"

My broader "outer circle" network comprises people in many different disciplines who are pursuing their career goals. I began to build my network in college with three or four members, and it has expanded to over four hundred today. I use every meeting as an opportunity to do four things: use my elevator speech to convey who I am, identify my career research needs, listen and identify how I can assist others with market intelligence, and finally, to identify possible new network members. When I was in job search mode, regular communications kept my network informed of my status. Ideas and leads rolled in, and I found my next position. My goal has been to maintain an active group of connections and give back, based on the principle of "How may I help?" rather than "What can I get?" I frequently provide similar career and job-search advice to my outer circle network.

With social media, there may be a more extensive network of loose acquaintances and people we feel we know, based on social profiles and shared interests or backgrounds, but whom we may have only met once or twice. People we loosely connect with at business gatherings, some current or past fellow employees, fellow alumni, and casual business acquaintances fit within this group. These connections fit well in the outer circle. This broader network allows you to research career alternatives, specific job opportunities, organizations, or industries. This group grows with every introduction you receive. Ideal candidates for inclusion are those with desirable career backgrounds, industries, professions, geographies, and work experiences.

Use every professional meeting as an opportunity to add to your network. Every co-worker is a potential network member. Every social occasion is an opportunity to identify and add members. In other words, every time you connect with anyone, ask yourself if you should add this person to your network. Researching alumni groups is an excellent way to identify potential network members. Finally, LinkedIn is the best online business networking tool available.

Networking Tools

An elevator speech is your brief professional biography, coupled with what you are seeking and suggestions about how the listener might assist you. Deliver this speech in a concise but informative manner. Practice your "pitch" with friends so that within two minutes or less your intended audience has a clear picture of who you are, what you have to offer, and the type of research or opportunity you're seeking.

Other essential tools include a business card, a résumé, and a LinkedIn presence. These are more fully discussed in chapters 7 and 8.

LinkedIn and Other Social Media

There may be people whose work you admire, but you have no links to them through your first-degree connections on LinkedIn. First degree connections include people with whom you have become connected by accepting invitations to be linked on the site. You can enter their professional circle by sending an invitation to connect through LinkedIn. Always include a message indicating your reason for seeking contact. If you have a genuine interest in the content they post (LinkedIn), images they share (Instagram), or opinions they offer (Twitter), you can demonstrate your interest in them by commenting, sharing, and liking their posts. Your profile then becomes visible, and they may choose to view it, increasing your exposure and further prompting them to accept your invitation. Think of LinkedIn like Facebook or any other social media site but focused on professional networking. The site allows you to research people with shared professional interests. Using the free entry-level portal can help you discover where your acquaintances are working and their connections, while allowing you to contact them via message. Building and maintaining your network is a lifelong activity necessary to progress your career.

LinkedIn has numerous networking groups, consisting of people with similar job titles, interests, geographies, and industries. It even has networks of alumni for specific organizations. The primary benefit of these networks is to facilitate introductions to assist with career development, market intelligence, and job research. Consider if you want to research working conditions and career growth opportunities at an organization in another city. The subscription model of LinkedIn makes it easy for you to identify existing and former employees of the organization and to contact them directly via the sites messaging portal to ask questions and seek advice. The benefits of these networks may be limited by members' lack of familiarity with you. There may also be a lack of responsiveness, but do not underestimate their usefulness for market research.

Profile guidelines on LinkedIn suggest that an all-star profile needs the following:

- Professional headshot with you alone as the subject.
- Professional headline that is compelling, accurate, descriptive, and more than a job title.
- Location—a city and state or region, not your address!
- Your contact information including e-mail, with optional phone number.
- An up-to-date current or most recent position. Describe the experiences and skills you acquired.
- If you have no work experience, indicate what careers interest you and why.
- Your education—college degrees (or years in college), certifications, and other professional training.
- If you are in high school, indicate what educational paths interest you, and why.

- Your skills (minimum of three). Choose the ones most relevant to you and your profession.
- Aim to have 50 connections comprising your "outer" and "inner" circles.
- Review profiles of people with similar backgrounds to yours. Use their profiles as guidelines for your profile.

Social recruiting is widely used by employers to find candidates, so it's essential to use it to your advantage as a job seeker. Chapter 5 covers this topic in more depth.

CareerBuilder recently conducted a survey and reported:

- 37% of employers use social media to screen their job candidates.
- 67% look to see how candidates present themselves on social media.
- 50% review candidates for a "good fit."
- 35% of candidates' social media sites show pictures of inappropriate behaviors.
- 29% of employers found positive information on social media that resulted in job offers.

Now that you've seen some statistics, you'll appreciate the power of these tools. Your branding is on display, so make sure your content is professional and error-free. Photos should present you in a favorable light. Remove any material revealing your personal life: for example, drinking at parties, political statements, or offensive remarks. Reach out to friends who've tagged you in a post to remove similar material. Some employers have HR staff who scan social channels to screen out people displaying undesirable behavior. Don't get cut in round one! Instead, use social media to highlight your skills and education. Include the types of career information you are seeking, and guidance you are asking about industries or job titles and any other helpful details if you are in job-search mode. Consider tweaking your privacy settings if you have any concerns regarding the available information. For example, you may not want your current employer to be aware you are searching for a new position.

LinkedIn and other social media are useful tools but are a means to an end and not a substitute for real connections. Face-to-face meetings have the most significant impact but are not always possible or practical, depending on geography or timing. Telephone or Skype connections are good alternatives. If using a video option, the rules regarding appearance apply. Be aware of the video background that is displayed, test the equipment, and practice how your image comes across with the position of the camera. Chapter 9 addresses video interviewing in more detail.

Effective networking is your most essential skill when researching future education and career choices. By following the directions outlined, you can access the knowledge and experience of others who have "been there and done that." Much of the advice received will significantly assist you in selecting the optimal educational and career path to meet your goals in life. Some information will not help you. Use your instincts or seek a second opinion in cases where you doubt the usefulness of some advice.

KEY TAKEAWAYS

- Networking is the best way to identify and connect with advisors for your career and education research. It is also the most effective method to find a job.
- Building and maintaining your network is a lifelong activity. Adding new and interesting people, while removing others who are no longer relevant to your professional life ensures your network is a resource to provide you market intelligence.
- A mentor who knows you and provides expert advice and constructive criticism is an invaluable asset. Networking is the way to identify and secure a mentor.
- Develop your "inner circle" or advisory board of advisors to help you examine career alternatives. This group is a sounding board for new career-related ideas for all the members.
- A LinkedIn presence is essential to networking. The site provides up-to-date career-related intelligence on millions of participants.
- Use of all social media for professional purposes can be beneficial in identifying possible network members. Care should be taken to ensure your social media footprint does not portray you in an unprofessional way.

CHAPTER 5

OPTIMIZING THE USE OF SOCIAL MEDIA

Barbara Schultz

So, you think you've got the whole technology thing down? I bet you do, at least when it comes to posting on Instagram, navigating your way around Snapchat, or connecting with family and friends on Facebook. Let's unlock the power of all the tools available in the palm of your hand and unleash them for job search.

Step one is to transform your social media skills from personal to business use. Leveraging social media for professional purposes:

- Promotes your online professional presence
- Offers a universal meeting place for efficient and effective networking
- Provides unlimited access to data regarding potential employers, interviewers, and industries
- On-line Presence

First, you'll need to do a makeover of your online presence before you venture into the world of networking. It's time to graduate from your high school yearbook page to a professional image and launch the next chapter of your life.

The branding process starts with some real soul-searching to determine what value and experience you bring to an organization, the things you're passionate about, and then explore target opportunities that match. Reid Hoffman, founder of LinkedIn and author of *The Start Up of You*, refers to "assets, aspirations and reaction to markets" as

45

"pieces of the puzzle (that) inform your direction and competitive advantage." Applying these three principles to your personal profile serve as building blocks to create a brand.

1. Discover Your Assets with Career Assessment Tools

Success in your career will depend on bringing value to your employer. And, the value will be directly connected to the skills, knowledge, strengths, and social capital you bring and how you'll use them. For many job seekers, it's a struggle to put assets into words. Consider investing in tools to help articulate what you have to offer.

And by invest I'm primarily talking about an investment of more time than money. There are many assessment tools available online that are easy to use and are low cost or no cost. A few options include:

- The "Career Exploration Inventory" available at jist.emcp. com. This guide goes beyond an assessment and includes a framework for an action plan. It's a tool that explores work, learning experiences and leisure activities to help plan a career.
- CliftonStrengths assessment (gallupstrengthscenter.com). This is a classic online assessment that offers insights into your unique strengths.
- Jobquiz.com (free). This site offers a career aptitude test and aligns results with your needs and ambitions.
- MyNextMove.org (free). My Next Move matches careers available within industry sectors and links them to your interests and training.

By completing one of these assessments, you've now made it much easier to script your content on various social platforms.

2. Better Understand Your Aspirations by Seeking Feedback

Ask select friends and family members to describe you and jot down their observations. Look for common themes with their answers and see how/if they match your perceptions. Make a list of classes that you excel in and/or find interesting. Consider the things you like to do outside of school. Think about topics you talk about, what stories you follow online, and books you read. Are you an introvert and happy with your own company or are you a social animal who seeks the company of others? What motivates you and will make for a happy work life?

Spend time on this to build the foundation of your brand. Matching other people's perceptions to yours gets you to a place of authenticity. Branding is so much more than just promoting an image—the picture you have of yourself also has to be grounded in reality. You can then build your profile by expressing the type of work you're interested in, as well as the kind of culture you're seeking.

3. Build a Great Online Presence and be Aware of Market Realities

There's always a shot of reality that must be stated, so here it goes: *always* be mindful of what the market will bear. No matter how much swag you possess with social media, keep an eye on the job market influences: your geography, the economy, and technology. For example, be realistic about the number of jobs available where you live and what level of compensation is possible. Jobs in New York City command a higher salary than Alton, IL. (and where exactly is Alton? ... that would be my point.) Unemployment rates are at a record low, which is great for job seekers, but don't expect that trend to last forever. Technology has and will change the workplace in the most dramatic way, so keep up with changes.

Networking and Social Capital

Social media platforms provide the opportunity to plug into a virtual community that may lead to real-life connections. LinkedIn, Twitter, Pinterest, and others provide a means to an end, but are not *the* end. In other words, rooting around the internet to gather data, sending messages, or building a profile are all necessary activities, but are passive. Getting a job will involve human interaction and building some real, live connections—a task that even more experienced job seekers find difficult to start if it means leaving their comfort zone.

Statistically speaking, participants in a survey conducted by Lou Adler, CEO and author of *The Essential Guide for Hiring*, indicated that 85% of job offers are made as a result of networking. An effective job search involves picking up the phone, meeting people, and putting yourself out there.

Regarding networking, there may be more receiving than giving on your part at the onset of your career. A life well-lived is one in which there is reciprocity. As you make your way in the world, value the relationships that you have established. Start by saying thank you every time someone helps you, be generous in sharing ideas, try assisting a fellow student or co-worker even if there isn't anything in it for you. Stay in touch. There is nothing worse than asking someone for help years later when you didn't bother to see if they were dead or alive along the way. Networking involves reciprocity. A big mistake that all but the savviest of networkers make is firing up connections only when they're looking for a job. You need to always keep your network alive. You may not be looking for a job, but a job may be looking for you.

What is social capital? Plain and simple, it's the asset known as the value of other people in your life. Traditional advice you may get from your school's career counselors often centers on transferrable skills and experiences. One of the real gems to carry from one employer to another is the people you know. The value of that galaxy of connections may not be apparent now, but over time, it will translate to employee referrals, warm sales prospects, and reputable vendors—a great cache of goodies to offer your new boss. Right now, other people (your connections) are the best path to your first job.

Information and More Information

You can access information anywhere, anytime, so take advantage of every form of media available (audio, video, and written content) to build your knowledge base. Be selective by accessing reputable sites. Always validate information by cross-referencing a number of sites to ensure the consistency of your data. The number-one question a hiring manager will ask you is, "What do you know about our company?"

There is absolutely no excuse for anything but a great answer because you've researched the company, its competitors and vendors, and you're ready. Draw a blank stare on the opening question and, guaranteed, it will be a very short interview.

There are also opportunities to become acquainted with the professional and personal backgrounds of those individuals who may be interviewing you or who could be your future boss. Any insights you can glean into their work background, education, and interests will serve to stimulate conversation and promote common ground.

Another important dimension of social media in job search is that you are able to acquire market intelligence about a company or the industry sector that they occupy. You can now conduct an informed and intelligent conversation with the potential employer, as well as build a fulsome view of the organization, to determine if the match would be right for you.

Don't discount the need to concurrently gather any intel from people you know who have worked there or have inside information. Explore any and all sources and don't rely solely on the internet if other avenues of data are available.

Top Three Social Platforms

1. LinkedIn

Consider LinkedIn the World Market of connections, with 146 million users in the U.S. and millions more globally. Picture a huge town square where people meet and greet, sell their wares, and share their stories, and you'll begin to understand the power of LinkedIn. It's a huge virtual neighborhood!

Here are some of the ways to navigate the "block party" and start the handshakes. Invest in a professional headshot. If you have favorite pets that are featured in all your Instagrams, leave them out of the photo shoot—your employer is only looking to hire you, not your pets. Next, put a really great headline together that captures the essence of who you are. Remember that recruiters spend less than a minute scanning your background to determine if your profile lands in the "Yes" or the "No" pile, so grab their attention immediately with interesting highlights. Save any job titles for the content section—they are absolutely needed to explain work experience but are super unexciting when it comes to creating the wow factor of first impressions. Use the space on your profile page wisely. Endorsements are good to have; recommendations are better. It's actually okay to ask someone for a recommendation and then send them suggested language. Assuming you would like to be portrayed in a certain way and your description of what you've done is truthful, why leave it to chance?

Use key words that get to the heart of your experience, because recruiters will use them as search criteria to find you. If your experience is in a particular industry and you want to remain in that industry, make it clear by stating "financial analyst in the *pharmaceutical* sector." The easier you make it for a recruiter to find you, the better. On that note, remember to indicate in your settings that you're "seeking opportunities" (unless you are currently employed and it's a confidential search).

Turn on the job alerts on your mobile app. Recruiters may be messaging you to make contact and will want to reach you within a few days. If you're not checking LinkedIn every day or have this feature turned off, you'll be passed up.

Make sure your résumé and profile are consistent. Keep them both current. There is debate if you need to attach a résumé to a profile as you may be repeating content unnecessarily. My personal preference as a recruiter is to attach the résumé so I can pull it up and share it with a Hiring Manager. If you are doing some maintenance on your profile, turn off the activity broadcast notification in your privacy settings, otherwise every single change (even adding a comma or a space) will be sent out to your network.

Keep your connections strong. If you are just stockpiling people to add to your headcount, you're missing the point. Staying in touch can be as simple as sending a quick note to acknowledge someone's work anniversary.

Get inspired by what others have done by searching profiles of people who you'd like to emulate. There's no need to reinvent the wheel; there are plenty of awesome profiles out there that you can learn from, just take some time to look.

2. Facebook

Recruiters are looking for you and may be using Facebook to find you. That's right, HR is refocusing energy on this often-overlooked recruiting platform, so get ready for them when they come. They have woken up to the fact that Facebook has totally captured the market with 2.38 billion active monthly users. This may be a social channel abandoned in favor of a more popular site, but you may want to consider coming back into the fold.

Facebook may also be useful as it represents a gathering place of family and friends who you can easily notify with a simple announcement of your job search. Take it one step further and let your friends know what kind of job you're looking for, so they know how to help you.

Facebook can promote your image by adding color and context to who you are outside of work or school. Of course, some Facebook pages should be relegated to the Witness Protection Program and present an image you don't want your future employer to see. Be discerning in pictures you post, comments you make, avoid anything controversial like politics, religion, etc. HR departments specifically troll pages of candidates who've made it to the final round to see how they present themselves through words and images.

3. Instagram

This social channel has more limited use for some job seekers, because the medium is photos and videos. For job seekers who have audio/visual (still or motion) portfolios, it's a great place to display your talent and creativity.

Similar to Facebook, you'll want to keep your personal life separate as you start to build a professional life. Consider setting up a secondary account, using your legal name to make it easy to search. Settings should be switched to "public" to allow for maximum exposure. Take it a step further and use hashtags with your post that are super specific to your subject area, but don't go crazy with every related hashtag that pops into your head—it's not effective and, even worse, can be viewed as annoying. Just search the popular tags in Instagram and use two or three max.

KEY TAKEAWAYS

- As a first step, you'll need to identify what you have to offer an employer, your interests and passions as well as the jobs and compensation available on the market.
- Take full advantage of any free promotional opportunities available on social media.
- Consider social media as a great tool to establish connections, but also one to use in tandem with human connections.
- Use the social platforms that align with your background, education and interests and then learn how to optimize the features on LinkedIn, Instagram, and Facebook.

CHAPTER 6

CREATING AN OFFLINE BRAND FOR CAREER SUCCESS

Kimberly White

The importance of branding and brand consistency was once associated only with businesses. Today, branding applies equally to individuals. It's inclusive of your "image" as well as any personal information—for better or worse—that may be publicly available to others. It's important to take ownership of your brand, because you, and you alone, are responsible for it.

Whether you're seeking employment or settling into a new job, consider the following aspects of your personal branding.

First Impressions

It's human nature to size one another up. However, the fashion and speed in which we make judgments may surprise you. There are numerous scientific studies on how rapidly humans form impressions about each other, and the conclusions are similar: it occurs in the blink of an eye.

One of the most consistently cited studies was conducted in the early 1990s by Nalini Ambady and Robert Rosenthal, both then at Stanford University in California. The scientists asked volunteers to rate teachers on traits including competence, confidence, and honesty after watching two-, five- or 10-second silent clips of their performance. The scores successfully predicted the teachers' end of semester evaluations, and two-second judgments were as accurate as those given more time. A similarly and equally cited study compared people's opinions of election candidates formed from brief glimpses of their photographs to actual election results. The accuracy was alarming.

Science continues to reveal that before we can finish blinking our eyes, we've already made critical decisions about someone we've only just encountered for the first time. Not only do we make split-second judgments of character traits like trustworthiness and competence, these impressions are often correct.

Of course, these snap judgments can also wreak havoc. This phenomenon of "thin-slicing"—relying on the thinnest slices of evidence to form opinions—is also how biases of race and sex are formed. While all job candidates deserve the same treatment and the same attention to factors other than race or appearance, we know that unconscious bias is all too real and that initial impressions can be terribly wrong or unfair. I share this with you because it's a hard fact ... and perhaps to make you more aware of your *own* snap judgments.[7]

While you can't control every conclusion that someone may draw about you, there are some steps you can take to improve your chances of making a good impression. Here are some tried and true tips for putting your best foot forward in person, particularly when it counts the most—during the hiring process:

- Dress to impress and err on the side of professional. As tempting as it may be to show off your personality with your unique sartorial flair, a neat and clean appearance always sends the right message. If you've recently started a new job or are in line for a promotion and you know your wardrobe isn't up to snuff, invite someone whose style you respect to help you sort through your wardrobe or even go shopping with you.
- Think about your body language. The right body language can show confidence and poise, while the wrong body language can sour how you're perceived. (More on this below.)
- Do your homework. I can't stress enough how important it is to know the basic facts about the company with which you're interviewing or networking. Don't ask questions that you could have answered yourself by spending 10 minutes on the company website.
- That being said, *do* ask questions. Come prepared with at least two questions about the role for which you're interviewing or

---

[7] For a deeper dive on this topic, check out Malcolm Gladwell's *Blink: The Power of Thinking Without Thinking*. Published in 2005, it presents research from psychology and behavioral economics on the adaptive unconscious that still rings true.

the company in general. An inquisitive nature is important in the workplace and valued socially as well.

- Don't trash your last employer. Talking poorly about other companies or colleagues comes off as immature and unprofessional.
- Focus on etiquette. Always stand up when shaking someone's hand or meeting someone new. Smile. Be polite. Don't check your watch. Turn the ringer off on your phone. (All things you've probably heard your parents say before!)
- Research the names and titles of those you may be meeting for the first time on LinkedIn (or ask human resources for this information) before your first meeting. Memorize names ahead of time.
- Send brief "Thank You" e-mails to people you have met interviewing or networking.

Body Language

Your body language is always communicating something. Whether you're in a job interview, a meeting, presenting to clients, or circulating a networking event, how you carry yourself makes a statement. And, in a critical moment, it can sometimes have an out-sized impact. In other words, if you fail to smile during an interview or when meeting someone new, the other person may assume you don't want to be there at all.

Standing and sitting with great posture—shoulders back and your head up—gives the impression that you are successful and confident. Recent research indicates that your posture also influences how you think about yourself. You are more likely to feel confident about what you are saying if you sit up straight. You end up convincing yourself you're competent by the posture you're in.[8]

Communication Etiquette

What you say and how you say it matters. Every person in this world, including me, has probably said something they wish they could take back. Do you want to be known as the person who speaks their mind no matter how hurtful the comment? Choose your words wisely and

---

[8] Amy Cuddy, social psychologist and author of *Presence: Bringing Your Boldest Self to Your Biggest Challenges*, has a famous TED Talk on this topic. While aspects of this talk have proven controversial, you may find her talk and her research useful and at least intriguing. You can view it here: https://www.ted.com/talks/amy_cuddy_your_body_language_shapes_who_you_are#t-29838.

carefully. If you develop a reputation as someone who is flippant, you may risk a friendship or the opportunity for a promotion.

Of course, not all your professional conversations occur face to face. Phone and email etiquette are extremely important—and often overlooked. While millennials often tell me they rarely use their phone for talking, knowing when to call someone directly can be game changing—or even career saving. Particularly if you have important news to deliver or are in the midst of challenging situation. If you're ever tempted to send an email that you think may be misinterpreted, pause and ask yourself if a quick phone call might be a better choice than an email or text. If you do decide a phone call is the right move, keep the following tips in mind:

- Always have a purpose for your call.
- Ask if it's a convenient time to talk.
- Keep conversations brief and to the point.
- If you have to leave a message, be concise and choose your words carefully.
- Speak slowly.

An often-overlooked aspect of phone etiquette: your voicemail inbox. Your outgoing message should be inviting, energetic, and free and clear of background noise. Start your voice mail by stating your name so the caller knows they've reached you and not someone else.

Here is a sample voice mail to consider: *Hi, you've reached Kim. I'm unavailable to take your call at this time. Please leave your name, number, and a brief message and I will return your call at my earliest convenience.*

When it comes to email communications, keep in mind the convenience of email is sometimes undermined by its risks. Far too many of us have "replied all" to an email that was meant for one person and one person only. And most of us forget how easily tone can be misread in emails and text. So, keep these email tips in mind before you hit send:

- Don't use uppercase or excessive punctuation, as this may indicate an unintended tone. Use bold and italics sparingly.
- Reference attachments in the body of the message so that recipients don't overlook them.
- Be succinct. Save the longer conversations for phone calls or in-person meetings.
- As mentioned above, be cautious when "replying to all." Make sure that the original email warrants a reply to all parties.

- Don't write anything in an email that you wouldn't say to someone's face.
- Always read your email before sending.

One more note about email, specifically your email address. Think long and hard about how someone might perceive you when they receive an e-mail from "sexymama1234@gmail.com." Perhaps your personal email shouldn't be *that* personal.

All the above may seem like a lot to bear in mind, and certainly none of us is perfect—it's easy to make the wrong impression. Keeping these tips in mind will hopefully help you avoid some of the most common *faux pas* that can tarnish your personal brand.

KEY TAKEAWAYS

- A first impression is made within seconds and your actions will determine if you get a chance to make a second one.
- Your body language should show that you are open and inviting, not closed and disengaged.
- Effective, responsible and respectful communication across all media should be the norm, not the exception.

CHAPTER 7

JOB SEARCH STRATEGY: TIPS AND TOOLS FOR THE SAVVY JOB SEEKER

Kimberly White

Many moons ago, when I was looking for my first job, I would peruse the classified ads with marker in hand, ready to circle every job that remotely interested me. Then, once a number of good prospects were identified, I'd start calling potential employers to set up meetings. Or, if I was feeling a bit adventurous, I'd hop in my car, drive to a prospective employer, and just show up unannounced. Job search seemed so much simpler then. Imagine a world in which you could get an audience with a decision maker without even having an appointment!

It's so not going to happen that way today. Like almost everything else in life, the effort you put into your job search will have a direct impact on the employment opportunity you end up with, so get serious, draw up a strategy, and organize tactics around that strategy.

Job search today has lost some of the personal touch. Technological barriers prevent direct contact with hiring managers, making them far less accessible than what I experienced early in my career. On the other hand, technology has afforded a much more efficient and effective process to submit a résumé (online), participate in an interview (phone/ Skype), communicate with the employer (text, e-mail, messaging), and conduct research (Google is your friend). I'll show you how to navigate the path from technology to human connections, so you can get in front of those individuals holding the power.

Use Strategies *with* Tactics

Getting the offer depends on building a strategy, coupled with solid tactics supporting that strategy. IN THAT ORDER. If you fail to organize your search that way, you're guaranteed to end up a hot mess. Many job seekers who've gone down this road before tried shortcutting the process and ended up spending lots of unproductive hours. Hate wasting time? Don't just apply to hundreds of postings and plan on doing nothing else, then expect to land a good job.

The most important first step is identifying what you want—direct your search and avoid applying for every cool job posted. Start with a targeted outreach by creating a list of select companies and desired positions.

Once you have identified a list of companies of interest to you, it's now time to do a bit more research. The company website is a great place to start and where you will typically find information around the history of the company as well as the mission/value statement. Does the mission/value statement align with your interests? Ideally, you will want to have a list of a dozen or so companies where you can see yourself working.

After your list has been created, it's time to put your toolkit together! The makeup of your toolkit consists of a perfectly crafted elevator pitch, detailed handbill and professional business cards. Résumés are discussed in chapter 8. With your toolkit completed, as part of the job search process, you are now ready to search job boards and access social media sites. Your end goal is to "land your next success," right? So, buckle up and focus. Job search, if done right, requires a significant commitment, so look at it as a full-time job. Trust me, you'll make your search so much easier.

Your Elevator Speech

Job search requires you to be savvy and adaptable as you put your marketing and networking skills to the test. The elevator speech provides a vehicle to tell your personal story in two minutes or less. Use the time wisely to share the most interesting and pertinent highlights of your background.

The elevator speech begins with a brief description of who you are, along with your skills and relevant educational background. It includes the role you're seeking, the industries you're interested in, and your goals. The close of your pitch should end with a request for assistance in your search, as well as your offer to reciprocate with help. Practice and become fluent so when it's time to tell your story, you'll be "pitch perfect." Here's an example of what an elevator speech might sound like:

"Hi. My name is Jane G. I have experience in IT desktop support, retail, and office administration. I'm graduating from college with a degree in computer engineering in June, and I'm hoping to find a job in IT as a computer software engineer at a company like Google or Apple. Do you know anyone in the IT field, particularly software developers who may be able to advise me on how to get started? Thank you so much for the help, and by the way, since I'm in IT, if you ever need someone to troubleshoot your laptop or install software, give me a call."

Here are a few more tools to add to the kit. They are not intended as a response to a job posting but are used specifically for in-person networking purposes. They should be given to people you connect with as a reminder of who you are and what you are looking for.

Handbill

Create a one-page summary of who you are and what job(s) you're seeking. A handbill highlights your skills, experience, and target companies. In addition, it details your wants/likes, e.g., how far you're willing to commute, specific industries that have appeal, if there's a remote work option, etc. You're looking to engage connections in your job search who'll be better equipped to give advice if they know what you're looking for. Handbills are also shared at events to expand your contacts and connect with participants you meet.

Business Cards

This is a cost-effective way to market yourself. Your business cards will contain all your contact information and can include your photo. You can get creative with a design reflecting your personality—but remember to keep it professional. Services like Vistaprint and MOO.com offer a wide range of designs and have easy-to-use templates. It's a simple way to make an introduction, plus it's portable, so people can add you to their contacts after the event.

Now that you've got your toolkit in order, you're ready to explore jobs. One of the first sources of jobs as you transition from campus to careers will be job fairs.

Navigating Career Fairs

Career fairs are widely used across college campuses and offer a great venue for employers to meet students eager to land their first job.

These fairs may likely be your first foray into the work world. So, get ready to transition from the comfort zone called campus life into the world of adulting. Don't worry, we're here to ease you in.

Career fairs have been described as a lot like speed dating. You're in a room full of potential employers and within a set amount of time, you'll meet as many people as possible to find a match before the time is up. Maybe you won't end up with your "person," but you just may end up with a great lead on a job.

Your great lead isn't going to magically happen; you'll need to understand the dynamics of a job fair. So, get ready to recognize a good match when you see one and then understand how to go after it.

Here are some tips and techniques to make the experience worth your time as well as the recruiter's time.

Before the Fair

Do your homework. Plan to attend a variety of fairs. Employers may be looking for a diverse candidate pool, so the process can feel overwhelming. Be selective in which employers to approach. Concentrate on industry-specific fairs, since you'll meet with recruiters who are focused on candidates in your field. Bring your "A" game, because you'll have a limited amount of time to grab their attention. It takes a lot of preparation before you step through the doors of the fair.

- Research the employers. In most cases, fair organizers advertise the roster of employers participating in the event—that's great advance intel to have, since it gives you time to go to their websites. Become familiar with their business, mission, culture, and take note of their current job postings.
- Prepare résumés and order business cards. Bring a sufficient number of both to distribute at the fair.
- Dress professionally. You'll hear about the importance of professionalism throughout this book and here's your first chance at making a good impression. When it comes to dress code, employers generally have a more relaxed one once you're on the payroll. Since you're not there yet, the recommended attire for job fairs is business casual. Not sure what that means? You can simply google "business casual" and follow the guidelines.

During the Fair

Take advantage of this free and convenient opportunity to showcase yourself to potential employers. They came to the fair because they wanted to meet potential employees, so they are ready and willing to talk!

- Demonstrate energy. Show you're eager to make a contribution and add value.
- Work the room. Have your list of must-see employers ready.
- Market yourself. What is your wow factor? Your elevator speech should be pitch perfect.
- Be confident without being aggressive. Good eye contact and a firm handshake are great indicators that you're evolving from student to employee.

After the Fair

You'll risk losing traction if you attend a fair and then wait for the employer to make the next move.

- Follow up. Within 24 hours, send e-mails to the recruiters you met, reminding them of your wow factor and expressing your continued interest in their organization.
- Send invitations to connect on LinkedIn. Your invitation list can include not only recruiters, but also fellow attendees. You've now started the process of building your network. Those contacts may lead to prospects now or in the future.

Career fairs not only provide employers a platform to showcase their organizations, they are interactive events for you to step out and demonstrate who you are. You'll be sharing your résumé and testing presentation skills as you introduce yourself. Some employers even conduct mini-interviews. Don't be caught off guard; practice responses and anticipate their questions. What a great opportunity to test the waters and sharpen your interviewing skills!

Employment opportunities can also be found online through job boards, search engines, and social media. Before you start exploring, make use of the following tools to streamline your back office. These tools will help you avoid getting stuck in an administrative nightmare. Here are a few I'd recommend:

- JibberJobber (jibberjobber.com): Manages information by tracking companies, applications, and network contacts. Can export data to spreadsheets and add hyperlinks to folders or files for quick access to information.
- Jobscan (jobscan.co): Compares your résumé to a job posting to show the degree to which your background fits a company's requirements.
- Jobscan LinkedIn Optimization (jobscan.co/linkedin-optimization): Compares your LinkedIn profile to multiple job postings to check for a match.

1. Job Boards

All but very small employers advertise open positions using job boards. The following list includes those that appeal to general industry sectors, as well some niche boards. As a first-time job seeker, you can certainly start by exploring the general boards. If your education and interests are focused on a particular sector, you may want to focus on boards with a narrower audience.   Keep in mind, not all job openings are advertised, so you should also visit specific company websites for up to date job openings.

Most sites first require you to create an account. You'll then indicate the parameters of your search, such as desired job title, and filters that refine your search. Filters will vary from one job board to another but may include qualifiers such as a targeted city/state, salary, company, etc.

Job boards allow you to upload and/or create résumés as well as submit an application on the job board itself, without having to go to the individual company's website.

- Idealist (idealist.org): Idealist is the go-to site for internship and volunteer positions within the nonprofit sector. This site allows you to search for opportunities based on your skills or interests.
- CareerBuilder (careerbuilder.com): CareerBuilder is one of the most well-known job boards. In addition to having access to job openings, you are able to upload a résumé to the site as well find meaningful career advice.
- Monster (monster.com): Monster, like CareerBuilder has been around from the beginning and offers the similar opportunities to search for jobs, upload a résumé and gather company information.
- Dice (dice.com): Dice is great website for job seekers in the tech

field to share your résumé, find salary trends and stay up to date on tech news.

- Glassdoor (glassdoor.com): Glassdoor's website has a lot of information on companies. Glassdoor is probably most known for its reviews and ratings from current and past employees, including salary information.
- USA Jobs (usajobs.gov): A career working for the federal government can be very rewarding. USAjobs.gov provides a host of opportunities with varied work experiences to find lasting employment. One thing to keep in mind when applying for federal jobs, pay close attention to what the application is asking for. The more information you provide the better.

2. Job Search Engines

Picture job boards on steroids and you get the idea of what search engines can do for you. They amalgamate websites, career pages, ads, and association announcements and bring them all together in one place, allowing for an even more efficient job search. Here are the leaders in job search engines:

- Google (google.com): Utilizing the Google search bar, users can type a job title and location and a list of job opportunities will populate for the job seeker.
- Indeed (indeed.com): Job seekers have access to company sites, online jobs and job boards. They can also upload résumés, apply for jobs and stay up-to-date with job trends.
- LinkUp (linkup.com): LinkUp is one of a few sites that share jobs that come directly from the company site which makes this site very popular to job seekers.
- ZipRecruiter (ziprecruiter.com): ZipRecruiter is an easy to use, mobile friendly application for job searching. Job search candidates can upload a résumé to the site. Employers can post jobs for free.

3. Social Media

Social media provides another source of employment opportunities. The same job alert feature should be turned on to get news of openings as they occur.

LinkedIn

This is the largest professional network on the internet, with 610 million users worldwide, 40% of whom visit the site every day. You have the option of passively searching by simply establishing a profile and letting a recruiter find you. Or, let recruiters know you're open for work by turning on this feature in the Career Interests section. From there, you can provide details for a recruiter regarding your level of readiness, type of work (full/part time/contract) and they will contact you based on your criteria.

Facebook

This is the most popular internet site, with 300 million active users, but until lately it hasn't been considered a contender for serious job seekers. Start at "Marketplace" then select "Jobs." You can then search based on job title and refine the search with additional criteria (salary, job category, etc.) It's incredibly easy to apply for a job within Facebook without ever having to exit to the website.

As of today, job postings on Facebook are limited and are primarily for small and local employers. On a positive note, there is limited competition for roles posted. Another interesting phenomenon is that recruiters are starting to search for candidates here—they recognize an opportunity with the large number of active users on a site not frequented by competing headhunters.

Twitter

This site offers a slightly different approach to searching for jobs, compared to LinkedIn or Facebook. While you can simply search for a specific company, you can also widen the net by entering a hashtag. Some of the popular hashtags used for job search include: #Hiring, #NowHiring, #JobOpening, and #Careers. Once you search those hashtags, you may have to sift through content that includes job postings as well as articles related to the topic, so be prepared for the hashtag to lead you to a variety of posting types.

After locating a job listing, there will be a link to the company or recruiter and, once you've moved to their site, you can then complete the application process. Another interesting feature of Twitter is that companies often indicate in their news feeds when they're about to launch a hiring initiative. If you're following a company, you could receive intel well in advance of the formal job posting.

Job search can be exhausting, so it's important to stay motivated and focused. Using this toolkit will keep your search organized and increase the odds of landing your first awesome gig!

KEY TAKEAWAYS

- Job searching is a full-time job. Treat it like one.
- Do your homework—know who is going to be in the room. Spend time perusing websites, uploading your résumé, and reviewing companies for an in-depth job search.
- Come prepared with your résumé, business cards, elevator pitch. And, of course, be appropriately dressed.
- Be interview ready–participate in a few mock interviews with a coach or trusted friend.
- Follow up with those you met with a quick email to ensure you stay on their radar.

CHAPTER 8

GET READY. GET SET. NOW GO!

Barbara Schultz

By now, you've assembled most of your tool kit and maybe even attended a career fair or two. Perhaps you've explored employment opportunities listed on job boards. You're certainly making headway toward successfully navigating from campus to career, but there's more to know and do. Here are a few additional steps to prepare yourself so you can get ready, set, and go to that first interview.

1. The Anatomy of a Résumé

The job search world is made of strangers who may neither be familiar with you nor fully appreciate what you have to offer. Understand the purpose of a résumé is to introduce your value proposition to the employer. Structure is for function. Use the limited space wisely since your résumé serves as an initial "calling card." Avoid a common mistake of even the more seasoned worker by simply recounting tales of a past job without demonstrating results or run the risk of creating an obituary rather than a vibrant résumé.

A powerful résumé does a great job of telling your story and is key to getting your foot in the door. According to the National Resume Writers' Association guidelines, excellent résumés are:

- Sales focused: Emphasize results; not actions. Quantify achievements with metrics.
- Relevant: Include industry/occupation-targeted information and

keywords.

- Visually appealing: Have a sufficient amount of white space and use professional fonts (Arial, Verdana, Calibri and Tahoma are best).
- Error-free: Perfect grammar and spelling requires that you proofread it to ensure there are no errors.
- Succinct: Be concise; avoid wordy phrases.

There is limited real estate on a résumé, so the length should match the amount of your experience. If you're a recent graduate with minimal work experience, a one-page résumé should be sufficient.

The basics of a résumé heading include contact information (name, city, state, cell phone number, e-mail, and LinkedIn address), with a summary statement that highlights your skills and experience. The experience section should include part-time jobs you may have held during breaks, campus jobs, and internships.

Your résumé must focus on quantifiable achievements showing the value you bring and should be expressed using metrics. Employers will be looking for ways you have made contributions to an organization, which generally fall into a few categories: increasing sales, decreasing costs, improving processes, and improving quality of service. For example, an entry-level accountant might state: "Member of team that reduced the average number of aged receivables from 90 days to 60 days by conducting weekly reviews of receivables, followed by soliciting clients for payments with phone calls."

Be sure to include any community involvement or volunteer work. Employers place great emphasis on social responsibility and will be more interested if you have shared views. It's perfectly fine to include extracurricular activities at school or personal interests (cycling, traveling, etc.) By including this information, you share additional dimensions of your life. These dimensions will also open opportunities for conversation during an interview and strengthen the human connection.

A chronological format is recommended as it's simple, easy to read and "ATS" (Applicant Tracking System) friendly. Although functional résumés have been used by job seekers in the past, they are not compatible with ATS systems and are not recommended as a viable option.

2. Understanding Applicant Tracking Systems

Gone are the days where your résumé is simply handed to a hiring manager. Understand potential hurdles in submitting your résumé and how to overcome them.

The first step in your job search may be submitting an online application through job boards like Monster, Indeed, Glassdoor, or through a company's website. In many instances, your résumé will be processed through a company's Applicant Tracking System (ATS). This technology is quite widely used: 90% of Fortune 500 companies use an ATS, with medium to small companies relying on them in increasing numbers.

HR professionals and recruiters like using an ATS because it makes an otherwise labor-intensive process much more efficient. For example, with any posted position, it's not uncommon for an employer to receive a couple hundred résumés for a senior-level position, and a few thousand résumés for an entry-level job. They'll likely see the benefits of an ATS far more than you, and here's why: the system is designed to screen résumés based on a set of programmed selection criteria. It works as a sort of matchmaker, searching for key words in your résumé that are the same as those which they've identified as important or required for the job. For the requirements, the system will have knockout factors. So, if a bachelor's degree is mandatory and there isn't one indicated on your résumé, it acts as a gatekeeper and won't allow your résumé to pass through.

Even if an employer doesn't have an ATS, job postings include absolute requirements, and if you don't have them, you won't be considered. Period. But when it comes to the list of responsibilities, an employer will look for a degree of fit. Employers may consider you a match if, for example, you have experience in seven of the ten items listed.

While there are over 200 different ATS systems that employers may use, many have similar formatting protocols to be aware of. At this stage, remember that human eyes are not being cast on your résumé, so you need to follow the formatting rules as the system is taking your word document and converting it into a digital profile. A formatting error could cause your application to be rejected simply because the system was unable to read it.

The Basics of Formatting Your Résumé

1. Follow these simple rules as cited in the National Résumé Writers' Association guidelines to ensure your résumé is ATS-friendly:

   - ATS will ignore content in headers and footers, so include your contact information in the body of your résumé.
   - Use the year or month/year when a degree or certification was earned, not the start and end date.
   - Functional or skill-based résumés are not compatible.

- MS Word, in general, is perfectly acceptable. However, résumés specifically created using the MS Word template feature are not ATS compatible.
- Don't include abbreviations for degrees or credentials next to your name (e.g., MBA). If you want to include a designation, spell it out, followed by the abbreviation, e.g., Master of Business Administration (MBA).

2. Use keywords and phrases that are relevant for the job, using these sources:

- Scan the actual job postings
- The Dictionary of Occupational Titles (occupationalinfo.org)
- The Occupational Outlook Handbook (bls.gov/ooh)
- O*NET OnLine (onetonline.org)
- Professional and technical organizations/associations

Sources of Information on How to Beat the ATS

There are a number of free online tools available to optimize the wording and formatting of your résumé and Linked In profile:

- TagCrowd (tagcrowd.com) identifies key words in job postings.
- JobScan (jobscan.co) compares your résumé to the job posting (watch JobScan videos on YouTube for more details).
- JobScan LinkedIn Optimization (jobscan.co/linkedin-optimization) compares your LinkedIn profile to multiple job postings.

What Happens Next?

Did you know that 75% of résumés are rejected because the ATS couldn't read them? Properly formatting your résumé and LinkedIn profile will allow you to get past the first filter. The ATS will then rank your résumé, matching it to criteria established by HR, and sort it according to the degree of fit between your background and the posting. If you understand how the process works, you'll avoid an employer's Applicant Tracking System becoming an applicant "trapping" system.

Because many employers require you to submit an online application, it's important to understand how that aspect of job search works. Please don't use this as your only tactic for finding a job; only 4% of new hires are found using this sole source. Optimize the online application process but spend the majority of time on networking—that's the only combination proven to be effective.

3. Preparing for The Compensation Discussion

Finding the perfect match is never a one-way street, so start thinking not only about what you can do for an employer, but also what the employer can do for you.

While money isn't the only motivator, it certainly is one of them, so be prepared to identify what you want for compensation as well as what you realistically can get. Start by building a scorecard that will serve as a wish list for all elements of compensation and benefits (i.e., the "total rewards"). Begin with the best-case scenario and check against the job market to see if your ideal list matches reality.

Step One: Identify Your Financial Needs and Nice-to-Haves

Let's start with what your scorecard might look like. Set up the list of compensation and benefits that are specifically important to you, then use that same card to compare one company's offerings against another. This is probably your first real job, and you may not even know what questions to ask, so use this guide as a start.

Total Rewards Scorecard

Compensation and Benefits	Company A	Company B	Company C
Base Pay			
Bonus			
Health Insurance			
Paid Time Off			
401(k)			
Education Reimbursement			
Fitness Programs			
Maternity Leave			
Paternity Leave			
Work from Home Option			
Training			
Mentoring			

In addition to traditional paid benefits, there are a number of other offerings used to attract and retain next-gen employees. Here are some of the most popular ones:

- Learning and development opportunities provide a path to progress your career and add skills.
- Flexible work hours allow options for start and stop times that fit with your life's schedule.
- Student loan repayment takes the burden of college debt off your shoulders.
- Social and off-site events encourage team-building and promote the employer as a good place to work.
- Positive social environments add fun in the workplace, from free Starbucks coffee to ping-pong tournaments to onsite fitness centers.

Step Two: Research Competitive Salaries for Positions You're Seeking

This is easier said than done, because many factors go into the base salary an employer will offer you. First and foremost, a company will determine their budget each year for payroll and their goal will be to stick to that budget. While they may have some flexibility in the total rewards offered, the best way to prepare is to do your homework well in advance of the interview. You'll then be in a good position to determine what competitive compensation is if/when they make an offer.

Visit sites that publish free salary information. Use that data only as a point of reference—don't consider it an absolute number that an employer will use. Note that employers each have a compensation philosophy targeting where they intend to pay within that range. As you gather data, you can then build a salary range.

- Salary.com is the most popular site; it also contains lists of benefits and a cost-of-living calculator.
- Glassdoor.com gives data on specific jobs in specific companies. Employees also comment on working conditions they experienced, which could be helpful in making an overall decision to join a company.
- PayScale.com provides a salary report that uses experience and education as some of the key factors. In its College Salary Report, it provides compensation information related to specific majors.
- Indeed.com is a job board that contains a salary search tool within it. Search both keywords and job titles based on millions of jobs.
- SalaryList.com uses official reporting by companies or the

Department of Labor. Data is organized by title, company, and state.

- SalaryExpert.com provides a salary report that includes cost-of-living projections and salary potential.
- Bureau of Labor Statistics Occupational Outlook Handbook (bls.gov/ooh) contains searchable salary data.

When you're reviewing salary data at these sites, make sure to get as much information as possible for the best match to the job:

- Job Title: Look beyond the title; the more important information is contained in the description of responsibilities. Be aware that employers do not universally use the same title for similar positions.
- Industry Sector: Positions are not paid the same across the board. Keep in mind which industries are in greater demand, as they pay a higher salary. For example, the energy or pharmaceutical fields generally pay more than manufacturing jobs.
- Geographic Location: Use filters that indicate the city/state where the position is located. Job markets vary widely when it comes to geography.
- Company/Revenue/Employee Size: The scope of the job is directly related to the size of the company, especially as you progress in responsibility.

Step Three: The Balancing Act

The challenge for job seekers is striking the balance between your bottom line (which you've already figured out) and the employer's bottom line (which you're not sure of). So, it's a little bit of a game between what you know and want, what the company is willing to offer, and the negotiating needed to meet somewhere in the middle.

If you've done the research and considered the overall picture of what will make you happy and what will meet your financial needs, then you'll make the right decision.

Note: Select states and cities have now eliminated the requirement for applicants to disclose their salary as a way to counteract bias. Historically, certain minority groups (women in particular) have been paid at a lower rate and this is a way to close the wage gap. Employers in states with a ban are allowed to ask salary expectations/requirements, rather than actual salary.

States that have passed the law currently include California, Delaware, Massachusetts, and Oregon. Cities that have passed similar laws include New York and San Francisco. The Federal Equal Pay Act makes it illegal to pay men and women different wages for the same work, and these new laws are in place to reinforce the equal pay act.

And One More Thing

Have a list of references prepared, with complete and up-to-date information regarding former managers. The list should include name, title, company name, e-mail (preferably business address), and phone number. It's optimal if you've kept in touch with past managers, as it allows for you to provide them a "heads up" that your prospective employer may be calling or sending a request for information. Your reference will be more likely to return a call or respond to an inquiry promptly if they have some context to the request. They'll also be better prepared to speak to your fit for the job if you can share an overview of the job description.

You may or may not be asked to produce a list of references during the interview process, but it's a great idea to have it ready. A future employer will eventually want to contact any of your past employers if they consider you a top candidate.

KEY TAKEAWAYS

- Be aware of how an employer's Applicant Tracking System Works; optimize the use of key words and formatting for your résumé to be accepted.
- Research competitive compensation and benefits data for the position you're seeking to accurately judge an employment offer.
- Take inventory of your financial requirements to ensure the employment offer will satisfy your needs.
- Prepare a list of references in advance of the interview.

CHAPTER 9

INTERVIEWING: HOW TO BE A "CHAIR TURNER"

Barbara Schultz

Think about one of the popular music/talent shows, "The Voice," and picture you're on a similar stage. You want to be picked in the "blinds" to get to the next round, the coaches don't know you at all, and you've got three minutes to win them over. Not so different from walking into that first interview.[10] Did you know that 52% of interviewers make decisions about a candidate between five and fifteen minutes into the interview? This is why you must do everything possible to make a great first impression.

An interview is not something that you do often, so how good will you be at it? The simple answer is not very unless you prepare and practice, practice, practice.

Before the Interview

First, gather as much information as you can about the job. Understand that job titles alone can be misleading. The more detail you gather on job scope, required skills, and education needed, the better you can gauge your background as a match. Job postings provide a good overview, but a job description has even more details if you can get

---

[10] Rachel E. Frieder, Chad H. Van Iddekinge and Patrick H. Raymark. "How quickly do interviewers reach decisions? An examination of interviewers' decision-making time across applicants." Journal of Occupational and Organizational Psychology, April 11, 2015

one. If you're working through a recruiter, they may be able to provide invaluable information about the type of workplace, growth potential, and nuances of the job. The recruiter may also have an inside track about the interviewer. Be proactive and ask for that insider information; the recruiter may not automatically offer it.

Next, do your research on the company. A common opening question the hiring manager may ask is, "What do you know about our company?" If you flash a bewildered look in response, the interview could virtually be over before it even begins. Go to the company's website and read the history; be ready to convey a basic understanding of the products, service, and customers. You don't need to be an expert, but how are you going to help an organization solve a problem or add value if you can't even clearly articulate the basics of the business?

The availability and accuracy of the internet information will vary if the company is privately or publicly held. In the public sector, there's a legal responsibility to shareholders regarding the level of accuracy presented on a website. While private companies will strive for the same precision in their website's content, the threshold for accuracy is less prescriptive. For private companies, validate information by checking multiple sites and look for consistency.

How employees are treated should be at the top of your list of questions about a company. If you know someone who works at the organization, phone them and just ask. Other places to investigate a company's culture are: glassdoor.com, greatplacetowork.com, indeed.com, and thejobcrowd.com. Employees weigh in on how they view the companies at these sites. Be aware that these sites afford disgruntled employees an opportunity to passively vent, so carefully weigh the reviews. You may wonder if positive reviews mean that a company is *actually* a great place to work. I was lucky enough to work for an awesome company, and people said that it was great on Glassdoor. Conversely, if you see only negative comments, consider that a red flag.

Once you've done your research and you're armed with those negative reviews, how could you probe them in an interview? Here's a possible approach if several employee reviews talk about the lack of training, for example. Follow up with the interviewer by asking questions about the company's expectations regarding a new employee getting up to speed, financial support offered to attend workshops, on-the-job training, etc. You can then determine if those complaints were valid.

Next, you'll want to explore a company's financial stability. This could be a little tougher to figure out. In the case of a public company, look for the 10k posted on their website. Depending on your financial savvy, you may need some assistance in interpreting the data. You can also simply google the company. An organization may be financially stable but could be undergoing turmoil with a merger or acquisition. Consider your personal threshold for the instability or chaos that could happen as a result of those changes.

What about a company's overall reputation? They may have no signs of closing their doors but have questionable business practices. Or, maybe they are dedicated to social responsibility and so are you. Press releases may indicate their good standing in the community or, conversely, can indicate a pending lawsuit, issue with a regulatory body, etc. Bottom line: do your homework to make the best decision.

Next, gather all possible background information about the people you're meeting with or may be working for. LinkedIn is a phenomenal resource to quickly and easily identify who you know and who the people in your network know. It's helpful to become familiar with the professional backgrounds of interviewers, as well as what they do outside of work. This personal information could shed light on their values, interests, and may identify common ground. Interviewers look to establish trust, so every time you strengthen that personal bond serves as a building block to close the deal.

Your résumé must be in perfect order, and your LinkedIn profile must be in alignment with your résumé. Prepare your list of references as well as four or five thoughtful questions. The questions you bring to the interview will likely be based on your somewhat limited knowledge of the company and the job. You can expand your awareness of issues important to a company by following them on Twitter.

As the interviewer is explaining the job, you should engage in active listening. Using this technique, you might say, "I hear you say that the job requires a serious commitment, and I've always put in the time required to get the job done. Would you need me to be on call on the weekends?" Make sure you and the Interviewer are on the same page about expectations. Don't be afraid to ask questions and also be a great listener.

Let's turn our attention from preparation to practice. Job seekers I've dealt with think they've prepared by just reading a list of frequently asked questions. No! Start by not only establishing a list of questions, but also writing out your responses. Avoid a situation where the first time you ever pondered the answer is in the actual interview. Take that same list and jot down the three or four questions you're praying won't be asked, then prepare answers to those, too. People lose confidence and especially stumble when responding to a question they believe will cast them in a negative light.

Find someone who'll act as the interviewer and engage in a mock interview. Ideally, that interviewer would be a trained professional (HR Representative, career coach, etc.), but is that realistic? Maybe not, so find a trusted friend who'll be objective and won't let you get away with a weak answer. Don't be afraid to repeat the question and try to answer it again if you made a mess of the response the first time.

Other options to prepare include watching YouTube mock interviews for overall guidance and tips, as well as accessing simulated mock interviews at virtualspeech.com or simugator.com. This exercise will serve as a dress rehearsal, and is time well spent. In fact, it's probably the most important step to getting interview ready.

Keep in mind that all the preparation in the world won't replace the need to think on your feet. Questions will be asked that weren't on your list. The most common type will be a behavioral interview, in which you'll be asked about a problem you've solved. Get to the point in describing the situation, explain the action you took, and report the result of your action to resolve the issue. Use the "STAR" interview approach that enhances your ability to articulate your story by framing the Situation, Tasks, Actions, and Results of your work experience. It's all about being able to demonstrate what you know, that you can communicate effectively, and the value you bring. Prepare for the interview by following these steps and you're much more likely to make it to the next round.

During the Interview

You've made it through the first round, now it's time to face the next one.

Phone Interviews

The first interview starts with a pre-screening prior to a face-to-face meeting. A number of candidates will be vying for the same position; getting to a reasonable number of candidates is HR's goal. Assessing the organization and how well the position fits you is your goal. If the job and company align with your needs, then the end game for this round is to move to a face-to-face interview.

The phone interview will be limited to approximately thirty minutes. If a recruiter calls and wants to conduct a spontaneous interview but you're not ready, don't even attempt it. It's perfectly acceptable to suggest alternate times. When setting up the call, confirm the time zone, the interviewer's first and last name, and company name. Clarify if the interviewer is an outside recruiter or the company's HR representative. It seems obvious, but candidates sometimes assume the caller is from the company, when they are actually an outside recruiter. Gather information about the company and the position well in advance of the recruiter's call.

Take the call in a quiet place—no traffic noise, siblings crying, or pets barking. And please do not use a speaker phone. As a recruiter, I can't tell if someone else is in the room and listening. Have your phone properly charged and be in a spot with good reception. Losing a connection in the middle of a phone interview is just bad form.

Have the job posting available and review the company's website if you know who the employer is. If the recruiter has set up the phone screening, they will probably just share generalities about the client (e.g., large health care provider, located in the city) but not reveal the company name. Have your résumé handy. Be ready to demonstrate how your background fits the job requirements. You can have the company website open during the call if the company has been identified.

At the end of the phone screening, the interviewer will indicate a timeframe for the next step. If the projected date has passed and you haven't heard anything, pick up the phone or e-mail to respectfully inquire about the status. Track the next follow-up date if applicable. Even if the interviewer indicates an urgency to fill the position, sometimes life gets in the way with shifting priorities or budget constraints. It may take some time for the search to get back on track. Don't be discouraged.

Here are the pros of a phone interview from your point of view. You're in a relaxed setting, because it's the setting of your choice. You can be sitting, walking, standing, it's up to you. You can also have notes available, drink water, or do whatever puts you at ease. The interviewer can't see your facial expression if you're anxious and no eye contact is needed. As the interview progresses, you'll be able to take notes to capture key points and/or ask follow-up questions. There's a certain degree of freedom when you're in control of the physical surroundings.

But there are also some potential downsides. Without the face-to-face encounter, your opportunity to make a connection is more limited. Treat this scenario like any interview and be professional, prepared, and have a strong close. Thank the interviewer for their time, make sure your questions are answered to your satisfaction, and get clarity on the next steps. Enthusiastically express your continued interest unless you really don't intend to pursue the job. Stay organized by tracking the details of your meeting by whatever method works for you—excel spreadsheet, Trello board, etc. There is also a free career management system that tracks contacts and networking information located on jibberjobber.com. You can even add hyperlinks to spreadsheets using this tool.

My personal turn-off as a recruiter is a follow-up call to a candidate who can't remember the details of the job. They might say something like, "Sorry, *what company* are you calling from? I applied to so many places, I have a hard time remembering them all." Remember, it's *your* job to keep the prospects straight.

Digital Interviews

While digital interviewing is not a household term just yet, it's quickly becoming a popular screening tool for tech companies, as well as organizations with high volumes of positions to fill and a limited time to fill them.

Let's be clear on what a digital interview is and is not. Picture a hybrid of a phone interview with a video aspect. This screening tool is referred to as "on-demand" as opposed to a "live" video such as Skype. The interview will be conducted from your home (or the location of your choice) where you record a session that a recruiter can view when they choose to watch. As for the job seeker, the recording can be done within about three days of the employer's invitation, making the time for you to "show up for the interview" less prescriptive than a traditional interview.

The actual mechanics work like this: You apply online and if your résumé is selected, you will get an invitation sent through e-mail to access the interview session. Questions will be presented to you in the form of text that appears on your screen. Simply answer the questions verbally while your video image is displayed; there will not be an interviewer on the other end.

Because each employer has a slightly different setup in their system, it's critical that you open the invitation and read through the instructions before the actual recording so you can be nimble in navigating their screens.

The next step is to literally have your house in order as it will serve as the backdrop for your session. This means you have a neat and tidy space to set up your laptop. Do you have a quality microphone? Is your video camera clear? Have you checked your surroundings for any background noise?

All the rules you already know about the importance of your personal appearance apply, but now add the dimension of lighting and background and consider how they impact your messaging. Conducting a screen test is the best way to see how different this setting can be. This dry run allows you time to observe how your hair, complexion, and voice either promote you as a candidate or serve as a distraction. A completely neutral backdrop is acceptable, but if you add wall art, objects, etc., make sure they support the image you want to portray. Look directly into the camera on your device and place your camera height level with your face or you'll appear to be looking down, rather than at the (virtual) interviewer. If it helps, imagine that there is a real person on the other end. The more natural and credible you come across to the interviewer, the better your chance of proceeding to the next round.

During the course of your session, each question is timed with a countdown clock located in the corner of the screen. As you respond to questions, the time visibly runs down on the clock. If you complete the answer before the time allotted, advance the screen to the next question to avoid falling into the abyss of a visual dead zone until the next prompt appears. Conversely, it's important to succinctly answer the question within the time limit so you're not cut off midsentence. You'll also need to get it right the first time as you can't go back to a question that you already answered. There is, however, a certain tolerance by employers for a total re-do. For example, in the case of a complete mechanical failure (e.g., your computer crashes, you have major technical difficulties), you may call the hiring company and request a second chance once you have your system up and running again.

The good news is that you do the interview when you want and where you want within the company's prescribed response time. Questions are standardized, allowing for a more level playing field. Unfortunately, you won't be able to gauge the interviewer's response, but you do have the opportunity to see how you come across. Actually, that's more than you would know about your appearance compared to a face-to-face interview or a traditional phone screen. By the way, some employer's websites provide an option to turn off your video image so only they can see it. If you find looking at your own image is throwing you off your game, then go ahead and enable that feature.

Digital interviews fall into a few basic screening categories. The first is traditional questions and scenarios in which you describe how you would handle a situation. They could include a more complex problem-solving exercise (e.g., write computer code for an app) where you submit the document online during the session. In that case, greater time would be allotted. In the unlikely event that you'd consider "fudging" an answer and invite someone out of sight to help answer the questions—don't. Companies have safeguards to detect that kind of activity and will disqualify you immediately.

There's no need to wait until you get an actual invitation for a digital interview. Do a dress rehearsal with an objective friend, using Skype or any other video conferencing app. This lets you test your equipment, see how your voice sounds, and check out your overall look and delivery. Your friends can provide constructive feedback to modify your presentation as needed.

By the way, don't forget to keep using all the tried-and-true rules of preparation for a "normal" interview. Prepare responses to questions that are likely to be asked, especially those that may be difficult for you. The less you leave to chance, the more confident and successful you'll be.

Video Interviews

This form of interview is simply a Skype or FaceTime session with the interviewer. It's a true hybrid of a phone screen and digital interview, but now you and the interviewer can both see and hear each other. Your ability to get your point across will depend upon presenting yourself professionally on a computer screen. In advance of the meeting, test out your equipment, including the microphone you'll be using. Conduct an actual Skype session with a friend who will provide honest feedback. How do your clothes look? Do your gestures appear natural? Are you smiling at appropriate times? Video interviews call for a much simpler setup than digital, but also require a trial run.

One-on-One Interviews

You have now made it past several milestones and won the prized audition with your potential employer. Understand the selling process begins from the moment you step foot in the door. If a receptionist greets you, they are taking note of your overall demeanor; don't underestimate the influence this person has in shaping the perception of you as a fit for the company. It's not at all uncommon for a hiring manager to seek feedback from the front desk. Were you friendly and positive when you arrived? Did you treat people in the lobby with respect? When told that the interviewer might be a few minutes late, were you rude or impatient?

This phase of the process is primarily about what you can do for the employer. Turn off your mobile device, greet the interviewer with a firm handshake, and maintain eye contact. Display good energy and be as natural as possible. A genuine smile and natural gestures go a long way in getting your point across. Bring copies of your résumé and a list of references with contact information. Ask permission to take notes, but keep it to a minimum.

Assuming that you've done your homework, you're now ready to listen to the employer's needs and articulate precisely how you will bring value, resolve problems, and provide new insights and perspectives.

Answer the questions asked with precision. You'll be able to do this because you've already conducted mock interviews, anticipated the potential questions, and practiced your responses. Seek clarity if you're not certain of the question being asked. So, for example, if the interviewer indicates a need to "fix their accounting system because they spent a lot of money and it's not working the way they wanted," you could ask, "Which systems are causing a problem? Accounts Payable/ Receivable, General Ledger? Who was the vendor? Was it cumbersome to use the system, i.e., not user-friendly?" Don't just assume you know what the problem is. Without some background information, you won't be able to relate your experiences and offer your solutions

Another situation where an interview can derail is the dead silence that sometimes occurs after you've answered a question. Because it feels uncomfortable, you may want to fill the gap and continue to explain your point of view. Don't—you'll likely just ramble and not add anything of substance. Instead, ask the interviewer if you've sufficiently answered the question and if not, offer to provide more information. If there was a pause, the interviewer was probably gathering their thoughts and you've now provided a pathway to move on to the next question.

Be clear about what role you played in any previous work or school situation; don't underplay or overstate. For example, if you were a member of a team or the team lead, explain the contributions you made specifically within that role. There may be areas of responsibility where you don't have experience—few candidates will be an exact match. State what you know and address how you will get up to speed to close any knowledge gaps. Employers will be looking not only for past experience, but also for potential.

If you are a student with limited work experience, discuss any part-time jobs you've held and the applicability of what you've done to the job you are applying for. If you can draw a parallel to any extracurricular or volunteer experiences, along with skills demonstrated there, you will grab the attention of the interviewer. Always show a willingness to learn.

Keep in mind that the meeting is a two-way street. Your mission is also to assess the fit of this position and company to your career goals. Understand that this is not the time to approach a compensation and benefits discussion, but rather to explore the company. This can include professional development opportunities, more in-depth understanding of products, services, clients, etc., to assess if this company and job meet your requirements.

Group Interviews

In this type of interview, you're actually in a room with fellow candidates, vying for the same job. The employer may use this process to be efficient and/or could be testing your ability to interact with others. If your gut reaction is to isolate yourself from the other candidates and remain silent, don't. Interviewers are already making observations of how you network/engage with others. Get to know the other candidates—just having an informal conversation may put you more at ease. Another benefit is that you may learn something from a fellow candidate and actually reference it in response to an interviewer's question. A common technique a company uses is to present a group problem-solving situation to determine team building and/or leadership abilities. The panel member will note if you give credit to others while building on other candidate's responses. Speak with purpose when it's your turn and listen carefully when someone else is up to bat. If you succeed in the group setting, you'll advance to a one-on-one interview.

Panel Interviews

A panel interview is when you're the only candidate in the room, but there are a number of interviewers asking questions. The primary challenge is to maintain composure because, let's face it, you're outnumbered by the company's representatives. The strategy here is to respond to questions posed by that one specific panel member while simultaneously keeping the balance of the panel engaged. Because the interviewers will represent different functional areas, make sure to get as much background information on each of them before the meeting to understand their perspectives.

When you enter the meeting room, ask where you should sit, since the company will probably have a preference for the seating arrangement. Eye contact and body language are always important, but especially challenging as you navigate your way around the room. First, look directly at the person who asked you the question, then as you provide more detail, expand your eye contact to others in the room and actually shift the position of your body as you include others in your answer. Great self-control is required as multiple interviewers want to get their questions asked and may be aggressive in pressing you for answers. Take the time you need, and you'll be able to control the pace of the meeting.

If you're lucky enough to solicit the help of a few friends, conduct a mock interview for a group or panel interview. Testing the dynamics of a group or panel interview in advance would be time well spent, as this is a different type of interview requiring practice with multiple "interviewers."

After the Interview

At the conclusion of the interview, you may be asked to meet with someone else, take a plant/office tour, etc. Make sure you've allowed enough time for this and recognize you've just advanced one step closer to receiving an offer.

Let's start at the conclusion of an interview and work our way backwards to what should happen before you even left that meeting. Here's how it works. Thank the interviewer for their time, express your continued interest in the position, and inquire about the timeline for their search. Next, ask if you may call back in the event you have additional questions (and you will have questions). Confirm a convenient time to call and verify the appropriate phone number. You now have secured permission for future contact and eliminated the dreaded fear of stalking the interviewer.

As soon as you exit the interview, jot down key points related to the scope of the job, and any open-ended questions you'd like answered. Most importantly, identify two or three areas in which the interviewer described situations needing resolution along with how you would or *have* handled them. If you're drawing from previous work experience, only consider examples that clearly demonstrate the specific role you played in adding value.

You had a chance to ask questions during the interview, but it's impossible to think of everything, right? And that's okay. In fact, it's more than okay because it opens an opportunity to stay in touch. Prepare three or four questions and call the interviewer back within a few days of your meeting. Here's an example of what I'm proposing: "You mentioned that your company website is not generating the interest you expected, and I thought I'd let you know some of the steps I took to boost my school's online presence. I did an audit and noticed that my school's website was mainly dated, text-heavy, and difficult to navigate. I helped my boss with a simpler design, adding better visual images. The one change I suggested that really caught her attention was to have more consistent branding across all channels to help recognition."

With this one follow-up phone call, you can secure a spot at the front of the candidate queue while others anxiously await a phone call. This is a great way to demonstrate your active listening skills, keep the connection alive, and ultimately land the job.

Consider all the possible outcomes if:

- An employment offer is made. Make sure the offer is in writing in addition to a verbal offer.

- A different job is presented. The interviewer is considering you for an alternate opportunity, and you may be asked to come in for another interview with a different hiring manager. Be open-minded and explore the possibility of an even better job.
- A different type of employment is offered. Budget constraints could be an issue and a contractor position is available. Listen to what is being proposed and see how it compares to your needs.
- A "no thank you" letter is sent and you are no longer being considered for the job. Send an e-mail or LinkedIn message to the interviewer and/or hiring manager, thank them for their time, and request to connect to continue a virtual relationship. Remember, you have a strong connection following your face-to-face encounter; take advantage of the opportunity to keep it going.
- There is absolute silence. If you never hear a thing from the employer, you have just learned something about their culture and have concluded this may not be a respectful workplace. Time to move on to other opportunities.

Always maintain the greatest focus on the hottest prospect, but also pay attention to other irons in the fire. There is nothing worse than an empty pipeline when your one and only prospect goes cold.

Don't be afraid to take a breather and step away from the job search for a day or two. Enjoy some physical activity, get outside and explore nature, or spend some time with family and friends. You'll need to recharge your batteries, do a postmortem if things didn't work out, and get ready to find your next prospect. If you do get an offer, congratulations and job well done!

KEY TAKEAWAYS

- Preparation and practice are absolute requirements to successfully nail an interview.
- Understand the different objectives for the "before, during and after" phase of an interview.
- Practice requires a list of potential interview questions along with your answers and includes conducting a mock interview.
- The setting and dynamics for every type of interview dictate the type of preparation needed.
- Be open to opportunities other than a job offer presented for the posted position. Other outcomes could include a different position, contract work, part time work, etc.

CHAPTER 10

JOB OFFER NEGOTIATIONS, ORIENTATION & ONBOARDING

Gerry O'Connor and Kimberly White

You've just had a successful interview, and it feels like you're at the finish line. After all, you've found the perfect job that fits your career plan; it's totally in your wheelhouse, with an awesome company and a great location. You want the job, and they've called you back for the final interview. Nailed it! Umm yeah, kind of, but not quite. You still have to get ready for the salary talk because that's what comes next.

Compensation Research

During some stage of the interview process, you may be asked about your salary expectations. Once hiring managers have narrowed the list of candidates, they'll often do a reality check by testing if what they're prepared to offer you is in the ballpark of what you're willing to accept. So, do your homework and research salary information before your next meeting. It's easy to do with several free surveys available online. Just know that free surveys will only provide general information and won't include the same detailed data employers use when they determine compensation.

Employers use several factors when matching jobs to survey respondents, including industry sector, company revenue size, geography, etc., and then make a judgment on the data by determining how competitive they want to be. For example, their paid surveys indicate salary ranges which they'll use to position jobs at the bottom, middle, or top of that range, based on their compensation philosophy and budget. So, while your research is useful for a general view of what an employer may pay, don't take the survey data too literally; use it as a guideline.

Two sites that provide comparative salary data for job seekers are salary.com and the US Department of Labor's Wage Earnings and Benefits page.[11]

For salary.com, enter the job title you're being considered for (or the closest match) along with the location. You'll get matches on several closely related job descriptions to compare your job salary with the market-based compensation data. The U.S. Department of Labor site provides compensation data by occupation, state, and metropolitan area. Selecting the geographic area, and then finding a closely related job function will give you the needed data.

Another source of salary data could come from your network. Do you know a friend, family member, or classmate who has worked in a similar job or for a similar company and is willing to share information or make suggestions of data sources they used?

The Salary Question

An excellent way to respond to an interviewer's question regarding salary expectations is to provide the market range of the base salary from your research. You'll also want to make it clear you're not only interested in the base salary but also in the "total rewards" package. Base salary only tells half the story. Total rewards include base salary, variable pay (bonuses, commissions), and benefits. A basic benefits package includes healthcare, a 401(k) pre-tax savings plan that includes an employer match, and paid time off (PTO) that includes vacation, sick days, and holidays. Combined, compensation, and benefits represent the whole picture, so carefully consider every element.

If a company determines you are THE candidate, you'll receive a verbal offer of base salary and an overview of employee benefits. If you feel the offer is below the market rate, ask whether there will be an opportunity to get to the market rate and for a timetable of critical milestones to get there. If your employer is agreeable, ask for a written commitment to review progress on these milestones at regularly scheduled intervals. During this phase, be very flexible with your negotiations, especially if you can't get a firm commitment to match your researched salary range. Respect that the employer likely has an established salary range for the position; however, they may have some flexibility with the timing to move you within that range.

---

[11] https://www.dol.gov/general/topic/statistics/wagesearnings

The hiring manager may also have some discretion with benefit offerings. Can you get an extra week of vacation, a flexible work schedule, or further work-related education or training? Can the company help with student debt or tuition reimbursement for future work-related studies? Does the organization have a formal mentoring program? A professional approach is to balance negotiating while continuing to demonstrate the value you'd bring to the company. Since you've done your homework on compensation and benefits, you'll be in a good position to discuss what's competitive in the market.

Don't forget; there's more to an employment opportunity than just a paycheck. Let the hiring manager know that you're also interested in future career possibilities at the company. If the prospective employer is unwilling to commit to any upgrades on compensation or benefits at the time of the offer, or over a future period of time, you have a decision to make. Accept the offer or continue your job search.

Once you've finished negotiating your total rewards package, you can verbally accept the offer contingent upon receiving it in writing. Only after you receive the formal, written offer should you assume you have the job. So be sure to hold off on resigning from any job until you have a written offer in hand.

Dealing with Dueling Job Opportunities

You received the written job offer and are impressed with the organization, your manager, and pretty much everything you've seen so far. But you've been actively interviewing and along comes another job that looks even better. The problem is, they're not as far along in the process, and they haven't yet made an offer. What to do? This is a great problem to have, but you'll need to carefully navigate your way through it. Consider the time it will take to chase down the second potential offer and how much time you have to formally accept or pass on the first offer. You can approach the second employer (who hasn't yet made an offer) and let them know you're interested in their company and have a formal offer from someone else. They will then decide to negotiate with you or set you free as a candidate.

Sometimes it boils down to a matter of timing. Employer #2 may be early in their search and not ready to make a move. Or, maybe they can't match the offer. In all cases, be thoughtful about the offer you do accept, understand the total rewards and opportunities for career development, and then commit 100% to the employer you choose.

Before Your First Day on the Job

Before your start date, you might contact your manager or supervisor to discuss work priorities, including expectations for the first 90 days on the job. Why 90 days? You want to hit the ground running and make a great first impression. It's a critical period that may determine your long-term career success. It also might (but does not always) represent a probationary period. More on that later.

Getting clarity on these expectations is the best recipe for success. Ask your manager or supervisor for detailed information on what you need to know before your first day on the job such as start time, documents you should bring, dress code, names of people to ask for, etc.

Orientation: Day One

Plan to arrive 30 minutes before start time, allowing time for traffic delays on your commute. Take a few minutes to review notes, check messages, and turn your cell to mute or vibrate. In other words, drop all distractions and be present. Be professional and respectful to everyone you meet. Show a genuine interest in getting to know people on your team—that's the first step in building strong work relationships and demonstrating your professionalism. Understand who all the stakeholders and key players are who you'll interface with regularly.

Depending on the company's level of technology, you may have even received a packet of information and documents via an intranet portal before your first day. In most cases, you'll spend your initial meeting with HR setting up payroll, signing up for benefits, getting an overview of policies and procedures, and discussing the company's mission and values. Orientation may also include meeting with IT to set up passwords, get a systems overview, and receive the tech tools needed for your position (cell, laptop, etc.).

Your manager may then meet with you and introduce you to teammates, conduct a tour, explain the job description, and maybe even take you to lunch! It's also your opportunity to ask any questions not previously addressed. The employer is eager to engage you as a new member of the company.

By the end of day one, you should have a reasonable idea of your manager's expectations for the remainder of the first week. You've met your coworkers, have gained some idea of your manager's communication style and preferences for how they want to be kept informed of your progress, and have had your questions/concerns addressed. You'll start to understand the company culture from your manager and teammates.

Onboarding and Work-Related Training

Onboarding is the process of integrating new employees into an organization and familiarizing them with the desired culture and behaviors. Onboarding programs are in place to ensure new hires are both productive and content. It can often involve many people throughout an organization, from HR to your manager to heads of other departments. Employers design programs that may last up to a year. They're serious about retaining and motivating you and know that they've got to grab your attention early in the game for you to succeed or you'll leave.

During this time, there's a focus on new employees acquiring company knowledge, values, behaviors, and cultural awareness to promote integration. I (Gerry) experienced a very successful onboarding program. It comprised a small group of new employees being instructed by more experienced employees on the cultural and behavioral traits needed to be successful. Emphasis was on teamwork, supporting others in their tasks, and leaving egos outside the door. The onboarding was highly effective at quickly allowing new employees to understand behaviors that were encouraged and helping to establish guidelines for new employees to work successfully with others. Depending on the organization, there may or may not be work-related training involved during the early stages of your employment.

The First 30 Days

The first 30 days provide a fantastic opportunity for you to stand out in your new role. You'll have the chance to make a positive and lasting impression with your manager and coworkers. Working hard and showing you're a team player will be well received. If you work remotely, communicate regularly with your manager and keep everyone informed of where you're at with projects. If you're on a flex schedule, make sure you are productive no matter your hours. Show your team that you're reliable, approachable, and collaborative. Learn by asking questions of established team members. You should also review your work priorities and seek guidance from your manager regularly during your first month on the job.

The Next 60-90 Days

Choosing to do only what your job description covers will limit you. Seek out projects that expand your skills, display your strengths, and increase your visibility. Often, the end of the workday permits time for more relaxed conversations and an opportunity to learn more about the job and the organization from your coworkers. Continue to discuss your work priorities with your manager at least once a month. Seek feedback on your performance and make any needed adjustments based on the feedback.

How you choose to spend your time will give your manager insight into your interest in the company. Are you signing up to attend social or industry-specific events on behalf of the company to network, bring in customers, or show your support for the company's mission? Consider looking into further education or training opportunities and certifications, all of which could lead to new skills that will benefit the company. How about joining a group of team members to volunteer at a shelter or mentor kids after hours? At 90 days, you should be proficient in your job, meeting or exceeding your managers' expectations, and building your network of coworkers. As you expand your footprint in the organization, your influence will grow.

Day 91 and Beyond

You're getting positive feedback on your work and building a good reputation. That's all great, but you've got your sights set on long-term goals like a promotion, a more exciting role, or better compensation. Start tracking your "value adds" to the organization and how your expanding skills will provide lasting benefits. Critical considerations when asking for a first-year promotion include:

- Researching career paths of more experienced coworkers. Were they promoted quickly?
- Are you receiving positive and regular feedback on your performance from your supervisor?
- Are you meeting or exceeding expectations, and are you adding value?
- Are you expanding your job skills and visibility, maybe by joining a cross-functional team?
- Are you seeking a promotion based on evidence you have earned it?
- Have you identified a company mentor who is advising and guiding you?

Probationary Period

Some employers include a probationary period as part of the terms of their offer. It's a trial period for both the employee and employer to assess the fit and generally lasts from 30 to 90 days. It's not a legally binding term that guarantees employment until the period is up. It also doesn't mean that, once you completed that 30-90 days, you're guaranteed employment until you decide to leave. And, as an employee, you're under no obligation to stay within that probationary period.

So, what's the point? Employers use this time to carefully evaluate you in the short term to see if you'll be a good fit for the long term. Equally important, probation often represents a waiting period for some of the employee benefits to commence. Make sure you understand what benefits you'll be entitled to within that period.

What Else Do You Need to Know?

Mentors provide invaluable career advice and may be available to you through a formal or informal process. Take advantage of any mentoring offered. An effective mentor will have company knowledge, a successful work record, and will be able to provide constructive feedback to help you succeed. Good interpersonal chemistry between you is a crucial element. That person will know the ins and outs of career advancement and promotion opportunities within the organization. If there isn't a structured program, ask HR or your manager to advise who might be a suitable mentor. You can also observe coworkers and make your call on who you'd like as a mentor—simply approach them on your own. People are generally flattered that you see them as someone "in the know," who you respect and whose advice you're seeking.

If you're in a small organization with limited upward mobility, then consider exploring jobs that broaden your skills with lateral moves into other functional areas. If your job is in logistics, and you move to a same-level position in operations, you are broadening your experience and skills. Employers look for potential in employees. If you can demonstrate the value of your expanded expertise, you likely will find that opportunities become available to contribute more substantially. Generally, the higher your value-added contribution, the more your employer will value and compensate you with increased pay and promotions.

Employers typically budget salary increases based on an annual cycle. They either grant increases at an official date for all employees or an employee's anniversary of hire date. In general, it's unusual to receive a pay increase before your first one-year anniversary, unless it was agreed to during the job offer negotiations. If a timetable and critical milestones were established to get you to a market rate, get regular feedback on your progress, and ask for the pay raise once you meet the targets.

Finally, if your employer is unwilling to improve your benefits or raise your salary to what research indicates is market rate, and you have gained the work experience you wanted, then it may be time to consider a move. Generally, if you do not have an opportunity to enhance your résumé with a promotion, added skills, or work experiences, or if you are under-compensated, consider a move. Now you've been around the block and can take all the learning you have acquired and use it to get your dream job.

KEY TAKEAWAYS

- Research compensation level for the position you are applying for.
- Consider the total rewards package, not just base pay.
- Make sure your job offer is in writing before resigning from a current job.
- Establish and maintain regular communication with your manager regarding your performance.
- The first 30 days are critical to making a positive impression on your co-workers.

CHAPTER 11

NONTRADITIONAL JOBS

Barbara Schultz

The work world is spinning on a totally new axis, caused by a seismic shift away from workers pledging lifetime allegiance to a company. Your generation is more interested in ensuring personal values are met than in making a long-term commitment to an employer. You want to make your way in the world but won't automatically sign up for a life of following rules in exchange for a paycheck with no questions asked. Today, you can start your own business, get a day job with a side hustle, or sign on as a contractor/gig employee. The reality is you can have multiple and concurrent types of employment. The easy in, easy out nature of entering and exiting today's workplace allows you to morph into a variety of roles.

For the entrepreneur, low barriers to entry begin with minimal start-up costs. The ability to promote yourself cost-effectively through social media further facilitates entry into that sector. If you consider opportunities as a gig worker, the threshold for educational requirements may be lower. Geography has almost become a moot point in the digital world. And, maybe most importantly, there's an entirely different perspective on the whole employer-employee relationship. You are simply not bound by the sense of loyalty (or fear?) that many of the more seasoned workers experienced with their employers.

How Do Different Generations Compare as Entrepreneurs?

Starting a business is relatively easy to do these days, due to exciting technological advances and thus the low cost of entry. However, there is certainly more to consider than simply the technology available, so I'd also like to dispel the myth that there is a virtual promised land of entrepreneurial opportunities. Let's consider the reality of economic factors driving you away from nontraditional jobs. Here's what's happening behind the scenes, compared to what's often portrayed in the headlines.

Headlines imply a greater exodus of millennials from traditional jobs than may be reality. Nonetheless, many of your contemporaries have chosen this road less traveled. There's always room in the world for the innovation and creativity that comes from stepping outside of tradition. If you're ready to venture into a world where you get to be your own boss, consider the following first.

Setting up Shop as a Business Owner

"You, Incorporated" starts with an idea that won't go away and that you want to share with the world. You may find yourself spending more of your free time pursuing that idea because you can't NOT spend time on it. The next step is to figure out how you can actually make money with your awesome idea.

Once you commit to turning your dreams into reality, you'll need to pull out that career plan you've written. Check your ideas against your plan and see if your passions, skills, and values line up with your desire to go into business for yourself. If the answer is yes, then it's time to move on to creating a formal business plan.

The business plan will serve as a blueprint and bring discipline to your concept. Start with a simple model:

- Business description: Can you clearly articulate what your venture is?
- Product or service offered: What exactly are you planning to sell?
- Market analysis: Who will you sell your products or services to?
- Resources required: What people, equipment, facilities, programs, and/or services are needed to set up and maintain your business? Do you have enough cash on hand?
- Competitive analysis: Is there anyone else doing what you're planning to do? Why are you different or better?
- Financial projections: How much money can you make? How soon? Is there a long-term need for your product or service or do you want to capture a short-term market?

As the idea grows, you'll need to invest not only time, but also money. Because you'll be bootstrapping in the early phase of development, you can use a variety of programs you may already have, like Microsoft Office Suite. You can also experiment with free apps like Evernote (to capture all your great ideas) or Google Calendar (to keep track of your calendar). Don't skimp on the essentials, like QuickBooks for simple accounting, which is a program you just shouldn't live without. Once you get a few sales under your belt, you can acquire better tools and may want to invest in resources to stay current in your industry. Whether your business is brick and mortar or online, your digital presence is critical. Start by building a simple website using economical, easy-to-use platforms like WordPress, Without Code, or Squarespace.

Don't underestimate the need to build a solid foundation for your business. Your mom or dad can't bail you out if you failed to understand the legal and financial responsibilities of ownership. Start with good advice from reputable legal and accounting professionals, because if you screw up the back office, you won't be in business for very long.

Calling in the Help Squad

You're heading off on your own, but that doesn't mean that you have to be alone. But consider who you reach out to for help—it's time to move from your personal squad of friends to a professional squad that offers sound advice and support. You'll save time, money, and avoid missteps by learning from people who've already been there.

A great place to start is a visit to the Small Business Advisory Center (SBAC) and it's free. SCORE is another free resource designed specifically to provide mentors for the early stage entrepreneur. As you develop your business, identify other resources providing expertise within your specific niche. There are also online industry groups available through social platforms like Facebook or LinkedIn. Find your tribe and start connecting right away; your networks will prove invaluable for information sharing, seeking thought leadership, and acquiring clients.

What About Funding?

Oh, that. Once you've made the choice to run your own business, the one aspect most overlooked or misunderstood is how you're going to fund your venture. According to Larry Jacob, VP of Public Affairs at the Kauffman Foundation, 81% of entrepreneurs don't access formal financing. You'll be cracking open your own personal piggy bank, accessing friends and family sources, and keeping a close eye on your expenses. Consider that you'll have both living and business expenses; make wise decisions to cover both. Maybe an extended stay at your family's home or living modestly based on the income of one partner? Unless you have some serious financial backing, sacrifices will have to be made to reach your long-term goals.

Millennials Who Followed Their Dreams

I sat down with some next-gen entrepreneurs who had the courage to step out and do their own thing, whether that was walking away from a corporate job, starting a side hustle, or supplementing a paycheck with a variety of gigs. Their pursuits span different sectors, including social media, higher education, apparel, food, home décor, finance, entertainment, and music. Some have since returned to traditional jobs for varied and personal reasons. Here are the stories of those kids who decided to forge their own paths by pursuing nontraditional careers.

1. Maddy Osman, The Blogsmith (the-blogsmith.com)
SEO Content Strategist and Marketing Consultant, connecting WordPress with relevant prospects from search. Started business at age 25.

Maddy built her first website in middle school, which may have sealed her fate in technology at the tender age of eleven. She completed a bachelor's degree in marketing from the University of Iowa, luckily debt-free. Her first "real" job was in sales at Groupon, but she discovered that marketing was where she wanted to be. She dipped her toe in the entrepreneurial pool by establishing a lifestyle blog and tested the appeal of her content before she took the plunge and left Groupon to set up an online digital marketing business.

She never wanted to be micromanaged and felt that being her own boss would mean ultimate freedom but discovered that having her own company was more work than she imagined. She doesn't regret it, though, as she reflected that 12 hours of working on what you love can't compare to eight hours of working on what you don't.

Maddy has worked tirelessly to establish herself as the evangelist of SEO and has enjoyed success in carving a niche business where people of all ages turn to her for her content creation and SEO strategizing. She was recently named one of the Top 25 Influencers of Word Press by Pathfinder SEO.

Best Quote: "Don't freelance right out of school. Learn the rules before you can break them."

2. Conor and Ryan Ashe, Common Allies Band (commonallies.com)
Entertainers/Musicians/Songwriters of psychedelic rock, folk, and blues. Started business at age 23.

These twin brothers completed bachelor's degrees in cinema and comparative literature respectively, along with certificates in entrepreneurial management from the University of Iowa.

These very entertaining young men began their love affair with music when they put a band together in high school and performed locally. After getting their degrees, Ryan worked part-time, teaching music at the School of Rock, and Conor followed his cinematic dreams by landing a job as a production assistant on sets for commercials. Both were soon disillusioned for different reasons. Ryan felt he was suffering under the hand of a blame-setting manager and Conor found the cold reality of life on set was little more than being a janitor, personal assistant, and gopher. When their dad asked, "What do you love?" and without hesitation they responded, "music" (twins have a way of speaking in unison from birth, you know), they knew it was time for a change.

To turn their creativity into a money maker, they had to learn the art of writing and negotiating contracts for their gigs. Next, they had to ramp up the frequency of their gigs, getting up each day to not only practice, but also to find new business. They also discovered that just plain talent was not enough. They observed other musicians who had crazy technical talents but had no clue about connecting with the audience. I've seen them play, and they are professional, humble, and respectful of all those in the crowd who are cheering them on.

Best Quote: "In order to make money, get over your ego and play every gig you can."

3. Pathik Bhatt, Former Founder of Raahi, Inc. (pathikbhatt.com)
Graphic design and custom apparel. Started business at age 21.

Pathik completed his bachelor's degree in industrial/systems engineering at University of Illinois, Champaign-Urbana, and took a series of classes focused on entrepreneurship and business. He then completed an MBA, as well as an MS in Business Analytics at Indiana University, Kelley School of Business. He didn't waste any time flexing his business muscle as he launched the sale of t-shirts and graphic design services through his personal network and a website during his undergraduate years.

His motivation for entering the world of entrepreneurs was simply based on his desire to expand his interest in design and Indian culture. He figured out a way to supply custom-designed shirts at a lower cost than others but underestimated the need for seed money to expand his business beyond its original roots.

He relied on a variety of sources for guidance, including a visit to the Small Business Advisory Center, and turned to family, friends, and a former boss to act as mentors. He serves as a great example of the new generation, able to transition from one role to another in a nonlinear fashion. He now enjoys a corporate position as Senior Marketing Manager at DeVry University, while concurrently involved in the gig economy by providing market research and digital marketing consulting on evenings and weekends.

Best Quote: "I didn't make a lot of money with my small business in college, but I look at it as a valuable experience investment."

4. Dustin Javier, President of Dean Johnson Advisory (djavier.com)
Financial Planning and asset management for medical professionals, business owners, and federal employees. Started business at age 27.

Dustin completed his bachelor's degree in economics from the University of Illinois, Champaign-Urbana. Although he did not take any entrepreneurial classes, his dad owned an Allstate agency and thus served as a role model. Dustin was one of the lucky ones who walked away without college debt and was able to launch his business with funds from personal savings. He was inspired to start a business because he sought a better work/life balance and wanted to provide exceptional service to clients.

Dustin has attained the certification as a Certified Financial Planner and stays connected with professional organizations. He also understands the value of paying it forward and mentors at the Philippine American Chamber of Commerce. Dustin is a grounded, serious solopreneur who has figured out how to run a business, get married, and have kids. Kudos to him on figuring it all out!

Best Quote: "I started my own business because I felt handcuffed at work and wanted to participate in my kids' lives."

5. AJ Castillo, Co-Owner of Americanos Restaurant (americanosrestaurant.com)
A full-service Mexican-American restaurant and bar in Chicago. Started business at age 29.

AJ completed his bachelor's degree in political science at the University of Illinois, Champaign-Urbana. He started to spread his entrepreneurial wings while still a university student, selling bucket hats. He had another gig as a restaurant worker to pay off student loans while he was attending college.

Once he graduated, he invested in a friend's food truck that turned out to be a money pit, but it proved to be a moment in time where he developed his hustle. He was living with his parents at that point and was under pressure to earn his own money, so he got a job at Quixote Restaurant, fine-tuning his cooking abilities. He then moved on to Firewater Saloon, where he learned what it takes to manage people.

He now owns a restaurant where he is the chef, in addition to managing 20 people and ordering all the food and supplies. It's a family affair, and his mom is the front of the house manager. He enjoys the freedom and can do things on his own terms. On the flip side, he sometimes feels the weight of responsibility and looks forward to a time when he can hang out with his friends.

Best Quote: "I follow Mark Cuban, who believes that you learn how to do everything from the bottom up."

6. Rachel Kremsner, Past Owner, ginger + bailey
Home and lifestyle retail shop. Started Business at age 31.

Rachel completed her bachelor's degree in retail merchandising, which included entrepreneurial classes, at Bradley University in Peoria. She started an internship at Target during college and started full time immediately upon graduation. In her words, the Target experience was almost equivalent to earning an MBA, as she rotated through all facets of operations: logistics working the 3 AM shift, managing HR, customer service, inventory control, and buying.

After ten years, she achieved the coveted position of store manager at one of the more successful locations, but always saw herself as owning a business. She had a passion for quality merchandise and interesting objects, so she created a formal business plan and took the plunge to start off on her own. Her husband played a large role in her success, lending his support, creativity, and technical savvy to get systems up and running.

She felt the keys to her success were that she embraced change, was analytical, and always had a strong vision of her goal. She also learned the value of social capital and joined the Chamber of Commerce, forming a strong bond with local owners.

Life changed when she became a mom and thus closed the shop. She remains proud that she took the risk, having no regrets about what she could have done, and departed her business debt-free. A great experience all in all.

Best Quote: "Be sure to have a good handle on your expenses and understand that you'll either have to get a business loan or find investors. Your personal financing will only last so long."

7. Andrew Schultz, Founder of Crimson Events (crimson. events)

Providing music experiences ranging from acoustic guitar to DJ sets to dramatic lighting. Started business at age 33.

Andrew completed his Bachelor's degree in business administration and management at Bradley University in Peoria. His love of music started in college, where he formed a band called Curbside, recorded two CDs, and played a number of gigs during school and after graduation. Like so many other bands, members got married, had kids, and moved on, but his passion for music and need for a creative outlet remained. He invested in DJ equipment and spent hours "mastering the mix."

He spent time honing his skills as a DJ in the hours left after his full-time job as Analysis Manager for NSA Media. The catalyst for turning his love of music into an actual business was an instinct that he could deliver a higher quality musical experience at events. After attending a number of weddings and listening to the music provided, he determined that he was skilled and talented enough to compete in that arena.

He understood the importance of relationship building from his days in the band, and always valued opportunities to partner with videographers and event planners, as they were plugged into the audience he was seeking. Andrew is a great example of "bootstrapping"—starting small and using every internet tool available. For the back office, he's invested in a low-cost business management tool called HoneyBook that handles the whole workflow from invoicing to booking. It's an absolute must to organize his side hustle as he continues with his day job.

Best Quote: "Don't seek the front stage. To be a successful musician and DJ, you need to be there for your client and provide an event they'll remember."

All the entrepreneurs interviewed were confident in their choice of pursuing their passions. While none of them is breaking the internet yet with fame and fortune, their success can be measured in the happiness they found in listening to their heart and choosing a different path.

Recommended Reading

My young entrepreneurs shared a list of personal favorites from their reading lists. I'm passing them on so you can also benefit from the collective words of wisdom.

1. *Why Now is the Time to Crush It*, Gary Vaynerchuk
2. *Will it Fly? How to Test Your Next Business Idea So You Won't Waste Your Time and Money*, Pat Flynn
3. *Side Hustle*, Chris Guillebeau
4. *IGen*, Jean Twenge
5. *Think and Grow Rich*, Napoleon Hill
6. *The Lean Start Up*, Eric Ries
7. *Scaling Up*, Verne Harnish
8. *Rich Dad Poor Dad*, Robert Kiyosaki and Sharon Lechter
9. *On! The Future of Now*, curated by Toby Daniels and Craig Hepburn
10. *The 1-Page Marketing Plan: Get New Customers, Make More Money, and Stand out from the Crowd*, Allan Dib
11. *Company One: Why Staying Small Is the Next Best Thing for Business*, Paul Jarvis

KEY TAKEAWAYS

- Write a formal plan or your great business idea may never get off the ground.
- Start small, utilizing free and low-cost advice, software, and online tools. Consider outside sources of funding as you grow your business.
- Your generation is motivated by a desire to pursue personal values, which sometimes feels in conflict with corporate business values.
- Work/life balance isn't guaranteed as an entrepreneur. You'll have to set boundaries with work and family commitments.
- Don't try to do everything yourself. Play to your strengths and hire or contract out where needed.

WHAT'S NEXT?

Thanks to all our readers who stayed the course with us on this long and winding road from school life to work life. It's not an easy path for anyone to navigate. We hope we have lightened everyone's load by sharing our work/life experiences.

We've covered several aspects of making smart choices for the future and would like to spend a few more moments addressing equally important decisions. Financial independence for you and your family is a key message but certainly not the only one. Getting off the family payroll is a great first step, but we're not stopping there.

We've also reflected on a number of non-financial rewards enjoyed over our careers. Each time you make your career choice, also consider the opportunities available for personal and professional growth. Seek employers whose culture and budgets support learning and development. The best employers help build your profile as a team player, negotiator, problem solver—all skills needed to remain agile in an ever-evolving job market.

Here's the bigger picture. Success and happiness in life can in no way be measured solely by the size of a paycheck or the importance of a job title. Success and happiness are life goals and will ultimately be defined by you; not by your parents, your counselors, teachers, or anyone else.

So, now for, the most important takeaway: It's YOUR life to live and you're responsible for shaping your future. That's what the world of adulting is all about. Lean in and take advantage of the help offered by us and everyone else in your life to launch you to the next stage. And, of course, enjoy the journey, every step of the way.

ABOUT THE AUTHORS

Gerry O'Connor received a lot of help during his career, including guidance regarding educational choices, career research, and job opportunities. He's now "giving back." Over the past 20 years, he has provided career and job search guidance to members of his professional network and volunteered as a career counselor and board member of the Career and Networking Center. Gerry is a global finance executive and principal of a consulting business (brentwoodadvisory.com) focused on designing and implementing organization improvements. He is an active angel investor helping early-stage businesses raise funds for future expansion. Gerry lives with his spouse in Naples, FL.

Barbara Schultz is a career coach and principal of The Career Stager, where she assists individuals to identify a career path and execute a plan at any stage of their work life. She's also a freelance writer, with published articles in *Society for Human Resource Management* (SHRM), *Thrive Global* (Arianna Huffington publication), and *Executive Career Brand*, covering topics from career advice to perspectives on intergenerational issues in the workplace. As a human resources executive, she's held senior leadership roles in entrepreneurial settings. She hails from a family of 10, loves to entertain both family and friends, and has been dubbed "Martha Stewart" for her over the top menus and tablescapes. She lives in the Chicago area with her husband, Marty, and has an undying curiosity about understanding what motivates people to do the things they do.

 Kimberly White is a wife, mom, mentor, and now an author. She is the executive director of the Career & Networking Center (careernetworkingcenter.org), a non-profit organization providing career support to individuals in transition or seeking professional development advice. Kim is passionate about serving the needs of clients, including millennials, more "seasoned" workers, and everyone in between. Married to her high school sweetheart, Benny, together they fulfilled their goal of "launching" their two kiddos, BJ and Logan, into successful and rewarding careers and weaning them off the family payroll within weeks of them graduating from college. She enjoys "doing good" in her community, throwing parties that double as networking events, and traveling. A devoted Kansas City Chiefs football fan, Kim is still patiently holding out hope that her beloved team will win another Super Bowl in her lifetime.

Made in the USA
Lexington, KY
14 December 2019